Nathaniel Hawthorne (July 4, 1804 – May 19, 1864) was an American novelist, dark romantic, and short story writer. His works often focus on history, morality, and religion. He was born in 1804 in Salem, Massachusetts, to Nathaniel Hathorne and the former Elizabeth Clarke Manning. His ancestors include John Hathorne, the only judge involved in the Salem witch trials who never repented of his actions. He entered Bowdoin College in 1821, was elected to Phi Beta Kappa in 1824, and graduated in 1825. He published his first work in 1828, the novel Fanshawe; he later tried to suppress it, feeling that it was not equal to the standard of his later work. He published several short stories in periodicals, which he collected in 1837 as Twice-Told Tales. The next year, he became engaged to Sophia Peabody. He worked at the Boston Custom House and joined Brook Farm, a transcendentalist community, before marrying Peabody in 1842. The couple moved to The Old Manse in Concord, Massachusetts, later moving to Salem, the Berkshires, then to The Wayside in Concord. (Source: Wikipedia)

Literary works:
Fanshawe (published anonymously, 1828)
The New Adam and Eve (1843)
The Scarlet Letter (1850)
The House of the Seven Gables (1851)
The Blithedale Romance (1852)
The Marble Faun: Or, The Romance of Monte Beni (1860)
The Dolliver Romance (1863) (unfinished)
Septimius Felton; or, the Elixir of Life (unfinished)
Doctor Grimshawe's Secret: A Romance (unfinished, 1882)
Twice-Told Tales (1837)
Grandfather's Chair (1840)
Mosses from an Old Manse (1846)
A Wonder-Book for Girls and Boys (1851)
Tanglewood Tales (1853)

PASSAGES
FROM THE
AMERICAN NOTEBOOKS
VOLUME 1
NATHANIEL HAWTHORNE

PRINCE CLASSICS

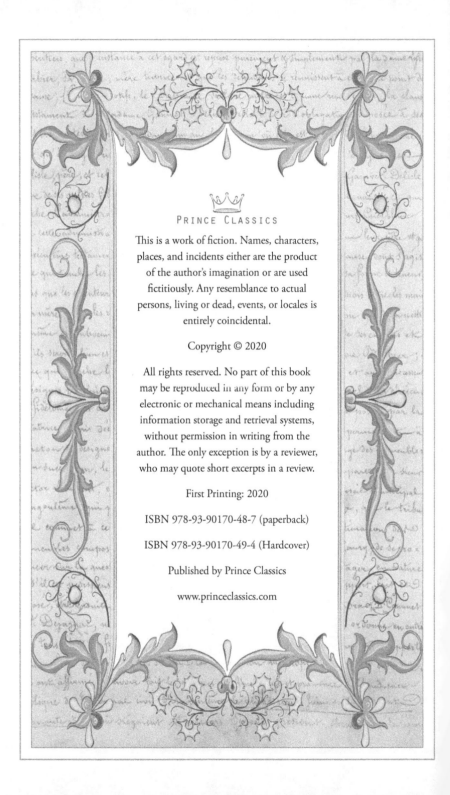

PRINCE CLASSICS

This is a work of fiction. Names, characters, places, and incidents either are the product of the author's imagination or are used fictitiously. Any resemblance to actual persons, living or dead, events, or locales is entirely coincidental.

Copyright © 2020

First Printing: 2020

ISBN 978-93-90170-48-7 (paperback)

ISBN 978-93-90170-49-4 (Hardcover)

Published by Prince Classics

www.princeclassics.com

Contents

PASSAGES
FROM THE
AMERICAN NOTEBOOKS
VOLUME 1

Passages From The American Notebooks, Volume 1

Salem, June 15, 1835.—A walk down to the Juniper. The shore of the coves strewn with bunches of sea-weed, driven in by recent winds. Eel-grass, rolled and bundled up, and entangled with it,—large marine vegetables, of an olive-color, with round, slender, snake-like stalks, four or five feet long, and nearly two feet broad: these are the herbage of the deep sea. Shoals of fishes, at a little distance from the shore, discernible by their fins out of water. Among the heaps of sea-weed there were sometimes small pieces of painted wood, bark, and other driftage. On the shore, with pebbles of granite, there were round or oval pieces of brick, which the waves had rolled about till they resembled a natural mineral. Huge stones tossed about, in every variety of confusion, some shagged all over with sea-weed, others only partly covered, others bare. The old ten-gun battery, at the outer angle of the Juniper, very verdant, and besprinkled with white-weed, clover, and buttercups. The juniper-trees are very aged and decayed and moss-grown. The grass about the hospital is rank, being trodden, probably, by nobody but myself. There is a representation of a vessel under sail, cut with a penknife, on the corner of the house.

Returning by the almshouse, I stopped a good while to look at the pigs,—a great herd,—who seemed to be just finishing their suppers. They certainly are types of unmitigated sensuality,—some standing in the trough, in the midst of their own and others' victuals,—some thrusting their noses deep into the food,—some rubbing their backs against a post,—some huddled together between sleeping and waking, breathing hard,—all wallowing about; a great boar swaggering round, and a big sow waddling along with her huge paunch. Notwithstanding the unspeakable defilement with which these strange sensualists spice all their food, they seem to have a quick and delicate sense of smell. What ridiculous-looking animals! Swift himself could not have imagined anything nastier than what they practise by the mere impulse of natural genius. Yet the Shakers keep their pigs very clean, and with great advantage. The legion of devils in the herd of swine,—what a scene it must have been!

Sunday evening, going by the jail, the setting sun kindled up the windows most cheerfully; as if there were a bright, comfortable light within its darksome stone wall.

June 18th.—A walk in North Salem in the decline of yesterday afternoon, —beautiful weather, bright, sunny, with a western or northwestern wind just cool enough, and a slight superfluity of heat. The verdure, both of trees and grass, is now in its prime, the leaves elastic, all life. The grass-fields are plenteously bestrewn with white-weed, large spaces looking as white as a sheet of snow, at a distance, yet with an indescribably warmer tinge than snow,— living white, intermixed with living green. The hills and hollows beyond the Cold Spring copiously shaded, principally with oaks of good growth, and some walnut-trees, with the rich sun brightening in the midst of the open spaces, and mellowing and fading into the shade,—and single trees, with their cool spot of shade, in the waste of sun: quite a picture of beauty, gently picturesque. The surface of the land is so varied, with woodland mingled, that the eye cannot reach far away, except now and then in vistas perhaps across the river, showing houses, or a church and surrounding village, in Upper Beverly. In one of the sunny bits of pasture, walled irregularly in with oak-shade, I saw a gray mare feeding, and, as I drew near, a colt sprang up from amid the grass,—a very small colt. He looked me in the face, and I tried to startle him, so as to make him gallop; but he stretched his long legs, one after another, walked quietly to his mother, and began to suck,—just wetting his lips, not being very hungry. Then he rubbed his head, alternately, with each hind leg. He was a graceful little beast.

I bathed in the cove, overhung with maples and walnuts, the water cool and thrilling. At a distance it sparkled bright and blue in the breeze and sun. There were jelly-fish swimming about, and several left to melt away on the shore. On the shore, sprouting amongst the sand and gravel, I found samphire, growing somewhat like asparagus. It is an excellent salad at this season, salt, yet with an herb-like vivacity, and very tender. I strolled slowly through the pastures, watching my long shadow making grave, fantastic gestures in the sun. It is a pretty sight to see the sunshine brightening the entrance of a road which shortly becomes deeply overshadowed by trees on both sides. At the Cold Spring, three little girls, from six to nine, were seated on the stones in which the fountain is set, and paddling in the water. It was a pretty picture, and would have been prettier, if they had shown bare little legs, instead of pantalets. Very large trees overhung them, and the sun was so nearly gone down that a pleasant gloom made the spot sombre, in contrast with these light and laughing little figures. On perceiving me, they rose up, tittering among themselves. It seemed that, there was a sort of playful malice in those who first saw me; for they allowed the other to keep on paddling, without warning her of my approach. I passed along, and heard them come chattering behind.

June 22d.—I rode to Boston in the afternoon with Mr. Proctor. It was a coolish day, with clouds and intermitting sunshine, and a pretty fresh breeze. We stopped about an hour at the Maverick House, in the sprouting branch of the city, at East Boston,—a stylish house, with doors painted in imitation of oak; a large bar; bells ringing; the bar-keeper calls out, when a bell rings, "Number—"; then a waiter replies, "Number— answered"; and scampers up stairs. A ticket is given by the hostler, on taking the horse and chaise, which is returned to the bar-keeper when the chaise is wanted. The landlord was fashionably dressed, with the whitest of linen, neatly plaited, and as courteous as a Lord Chamberlain. Visitors from Boston thronging the house,—some, standing at the bar, watching the process of preparing tumblers of punch,—others sitting at the windows of different parlors,—some with faces flushed, puffing cigars. The bill of fare for the day was stuck up beside the bar. Opposite this principal hotel there was another, called "The Mechanics," which seemed to be equally thronged. I suspect that the company were about on a par in each; for at the Maverick House, though well dressed, they seemed to be merely Sunday gentlemen,—mostly young fellows,—clerks in dry-goods stores being the aristocracy of them. One, very fashionable in appearance, with a handsome cane, happened to stop by me and lift up his foot, and I noticed that the sole of his boot (which was exquisitely polished) was all worn out. I apprehend that some such minor deficiencies might have been detected in the general showiness of most of them. There were girls, too, but not pretty ones, nor, on the whole, such good imitations of gentility as the young men. There were as many people as are usually collected at a muster,

11

or on similar occasions, lounging about, without any apparent enjoyment; but the observation of this may serve me to make a sketch of the mode of spending the Sabbath by the majority of unmarried, young, middling-class people, near a great town. Most of the people had smart canes and bosom-pins.

Crossing the ferry into Boston, we went to the City Tavern, where the bar-room presented a Sabbath scene of repose,—stage-folk lounging in chairs half asleep, smoking cigars, generally with clean linen and other niceties of apparel, to mark the day. The doors and blinds of an oyster and refreshment shop across the street were closed, but I saw people enter it. There were two owls in a back court, visible through a window of the bar-room,—speckled gray, with dark-blue eyes,—the queerest-looking birds that exist,—so solemn and wise,—dozing away the day, much like the rest of the people, only that they looked wiser than any others. Their hooked beaks looked like hooked noses. A dull scene this. A stranger, here and there, poring over a newspaper. Many of the stage-folk sitting in chairs on the pavement, in front of the door.

We went to the top of the hill which formed part of Gardiner Greene's estate, and which is now in the process of levelling, and pretty much taken away, except the highest point, and a narrow path to ascend to it. It gives an admirable view of the city, being almost as high as the steeples and the dome of the State House, and overlooking the whole mass of brick buildings and slated roofs, with glimpses of streets far below. It was really a pity to take it down. I noticed the stump of a very large elm, recently felled. No house in the city could have reared its roof so high as the roots of that tree, if indeed the church-spires did so.

On our drive home we passed through Charlestown. Stages in abundance were passing the road, burdened with passengers inside and out; also chaises and barouches, horsemen and footmen. We are a community of Sabbath-breakers.

August 31st.—A drive to Nahant yesterday afternoon. Stopped at Rice's, and afterwards walked down to the steamboat wharf to see the passengers land. It is strange how few good faces there are in the world, comparatively to the ugly ones. Scarcely a single comely one in all this collection. Then to the hotel. Barouches at the doors, and gentlemen and ladies going to drive, and gentlemen smoking round the piazza. The bar-keeper had one of Benton's mint-drops for a bosom-brooch! It made a very handsome one. I crossed the beach for home about sunset. The tide was so far down as just to give me a passage on the hard sand, between the sea and the loose gravel. The sea was calm and smooth, with only the surf-waves whitening along the beach. Several ladies and gentlemen on horseback were cantering and galloping before and behind me.

A hint of a story,—some incident which should bring on a general war; and the chief actor in the incident to have something corresponding to the mischief he had caused.

September 7th—A drive to Ipswich with B———. At the tavern was an old, fat, country major, and another old fellow, laughing and playing off jokes on each other,—one tying a ribbon upon the other's hat. One had been a trumpeter to the major's troop. Walking about town, we knocked, for a whim, at the door of a dark old house, and inquired if Miss Hannah Lord lived there. A woman of about thirty came to the door, with rather a confused smile, and a disorder about the bosom of her dress, as if she had been disturbed while nursing her child. She answered us with great kindness.

Entering the burial-ground, where some masons were building a tomb, we found a good many old monuments, and several covered with slabs of red freestone or slate, and with arms sculptured on the slab, or an inlaid circle of slate. On one slate gravestone, of the Rev. Nathl. Rogers, there was a portrait of that worthy, about a third of the size of life, carved in relief, with his cloak, band, and wig, in excellent preservation, all the buttons of his waistcoat being cut with great minuteness,—the minister's nose being on a level with his cheeks. It was an upright gravestone. Returning home, I held a colloquy with a young girl about the right road. She had come out to feed a pig, and was a little suspicious that we were making fun of her, yet answered us with a shy laugh and good-nature,—the pig all the time squealing for his dinner.

Displayed along the walls, and suspended from the pillars of the original King's Chapel, were coats-of-arms of the king, the successive governors, and other distinguished men. In the pulpit there was an hour-glass on a large and elaborate brass stand. The organ was surmounted by a gilt crown in the centre, supported by a gilt mitre on each side. The governor's pew had Corinthian pillars, and crimson damask tapestry. In 1727 it was lined with china, probably tiles.

Saint Augustin, at mass, charged all that were accursed to go out of the church. "Then a dead body arose, and went out of the church into the churchyard, with a white cloth on its head, and stood there till mass was over. It was a former lord of the manor, whom a curate had cursed because he refused to pay his tithes. A justice also commanded the dead curate to arise, and gave him a rod; and the dead lord, kneeling, received penance thereby." He then ordered the lord to go again to his grave, which he did, and fell immediately to ashes. Saint Augustin offered to pray for the curate, that he might remain on earth to confirm men in their belief; but the curate refused, because he was in the place of rest.

A sketch to be given of a modern reformer,—a type of the extreme doctrines on the subject of slaves, cold water, and other such topics. He goes about the streets haranguing most eloquently, and is on the point of making many converts, when his labors are suddenly interrupted by the appearance of the keeper of a mad-house, whence he has escaped. Much may be made of this idea.

A change from a gay young girl to an old woman; the melancholy events, the effects of which have clustered around her character, and gradually imbued it with their influence, till she becomes a lover of sick-chambers, taking pleasure in receiving dying breaths and in laying out the dead; also having her mind full of funeral reminiscences, and possessing more acquaintances beneath the burial turf than above it.

A well-concerted train of events to be thrown into confusion by some misplaced circumstance, unsuspected till the catastrophe, yet exerting its influence from beginning to end.

On the common, at dusk, after a salute from two field-pieces, the smoke lay long and heavily on the ground, without much spreading beyond the original space over which it had gushed from the guns. It was about the height of a man. The evening clear, but with an autumnal chill.

The world is so sad and solemn, that things meant in jest are liable, by an overpowering influence, to become dreadful earnest,—gayly dressed fantasies turning to ghostly and black-clad images of themselves.

A story, the hero of which is to be represented as naturally capable of deep and strong passion, and looking forward to the time when he shall feel passionate love, which is to be the great event of his existence. But it so chances that he never falls in love, and although he gives up the expectation of so doing, and marries calmly, yet it is somewhat sadly, with sentiments merely of esteem for his bride. The lady might be one who had loved him early in life, but whom then, in his expectation of passionate love, he had scorned.

The scene of a story or sketch to be laid within the light of a street-lantern; the time, when the lamp is near going out; and the catastrophe to be simultaneous with the last flickering gleam.

The peculiar weariness and depression of spirits which is felt after a day wasted in turning over a magazine or other light miscellany, different from the state of the mind after severe study; because there has been no excitement, no difficulties to be overcome, but the spirits have evaporated insensibly.

To represent the process by which sober truth gradually strips off all the beautiful draperies with which imagination has enveloped a beloved object, till from an angel she turns out to be a merely ordinary woman. This to be done without caricature, perhaps with a quiet humor interfused, but the prevailing impression to be a sad one. The story might consist of the various alterations in the feelings of the absent lover, caused by successive events that display the true character of his mistress; and the catastrophe should take place at their meeting, when he finds himself equally disappointed in her person; or the whole spirit of the thing may here be reproduced.

15

Last evening, from the opposite shore of the North River, a view of the town mirrored in the water, which was as smooth as glass, with no perceptible tide or agitation, except a trifling swell and reflux on the sand, although the shadow of the moon danced in it. The picture of the town perfect in the water,—towers of churches, houses, with here and there a light gleaming near the shore above, and more faintly glimmering under water,—all perfect, but somewhat more hazy and indistinct than the reality. There were many clouds flitting about the sky; and the picture of each could be traced in the water,— the ghost of what was itself unsubstantial. The rattling of wheels heard long and far through the town. Voices of people talking on the other side of the river, the tones being so distinguishable in all their variations that it seemed as if what was there said might be understood; but it was not so.

Two persons might be bitter enemies through life, and mutually cause the ruin of one another, and of all that were dear to them. Finally, meeting at the funeral of a grandchild, the offspring of a son and daughter married without their consent,—and who, as well as the child, had been the victims of their hatred,—they might discover that the supposed ground of the quarrel was altogether a mistake, and then be wofully reconciled.

Two persons, by mutual agreement, to make their wills in each other's favor, then to wait impatiently for one another's death, and both to be informed of the desired event at the same time. Both, in most joyous sorrow, hasten to be present at the funeral, meet, and find themselves both hoaxed.

The story of a man, cold and hard-hearted, and acknowledging no brotherhood with mankind. At his death they might try to dig him a grave, but, at a little space beneath the ground, strike upon a rock, as if the earth refused to receive the unnatural son into her bosom. Then they would put him into an old sepulchre, where the coffins and corpses were all turned to dust, and so he would be alone. Then the body would petrify; and he having died in some characteristic act and expression, he would seem, through endless ages of death, to repel society as in life, and no one would be buried in that tomb forever.

Cannon transformed to church-bells.

A person, even before middle age, may become musty and faded among the people with whom he has grown up from childhood; but, by migrating to a new place, he appears fresh with the effect of youth, which may be communicated from the impressions of others to his own feelings.

In an old house, a mysterious knocking might be beard on the wall, where had formerly been a doorway, now bricked up.

It might be stated, as the closing circumstance of a tale, that the body of one of the characters had been petrified, and still existed in that state.

A young man to win the love of a girl, without any serious intentions, and to find that in that love, which might have been the greatest blessing of his life, he had conjured up a spirit of mischief which pursued him throughout his whole career,—and this without any revengeful purposes on the part of the deserted girl.

Two lovers, or other persons, on the most private business, to appoint a meeting in what they supposed to be a place of the utmost solitude, and to find it thronged with people.

October 17th.—Some of the oaks are now a deep brown red; others are changed to a light green, which, at a little distance, especially in the sunshine, looks like the green of early spring. In some trees, different masses of the foliage show each of these hues. Some of the walnut-trees have a yet more delicate green. Others are of a bright sunny yellow.

Mr. ———— was married to Miss ———— last Wednesday. Yesterday Mr. Brazer, preaching on the comet, observed that not one, probably, of all who heard him, would witness its reappearance. Mrs. ———— shed tears. Poor soul! she would be contented to dwell in earthly love to all eternity!

Some treasure or other thing to be buried, and a tree planted directly over the spot, so as to embrace it with its roots.

A tree, tall and venerable, to be said by tradition to have been the staff of some famous man, who happened to thrust it into the ground, where it took root.

A fellow without money, having a hundred and seventy miles to go, fastened a chain and padlock to his legs, and lay down to sleep in a field. He was apprehended, and carried gratis to a jail in the town whither he desired to go.

An old volume in a large library,—every one to be afraid to unclasp and open it, because it was said to be a book of magic.

A ghost seen by moonlight; when the moon was out, it would shine and melt through the airy substance of the ghost, as through a cloud.

Prideaux, Bishop of Worcester, during the sway of the Parliament, was forced to support himself and his family by selling his household goods. A friend asked him, "How doth your lordship?" "Never better in my life," said the Bishop, "only I have too great a stomach; for I have eaten that little plate which the sequestrators left me. I have eaten a great library of excellent books. I have eaten a great deal of linen, much of my brass, some of my pewter, and now I am come to eat iron; and what will come next I know not."

A scold and a blockhead,—brimstone and wood,—a good match.

To make one's own reflection in a mirror the subject of a story.

In a dream to wander to some place where may be heard the complaints of all the miserable on earth.

Some common quality or circumstance that should bring together people the most unlike in all other respects, and make a brotherhood and sisterhood of them,—the rich and the proud finding themselves in the same category with the mean and the despised.

A person to consider himself as the prime mover of certain remarkable events, but to discover that his actions have not contributed in the least thereto. Another person to be the cause, without suspecting it.

October 25th.—A person or family long desires some particular good. At last it comes in such profusion as to be the great pest of their lives.

A man, perhaps with a persuasion that he shall make his fortune by some singular means, and with an eager longing so to do, while digging or boring for water, to strike upon a salt-spring.

To have one event operate in several places,—as, for example, if a man's head were to be cut off in one town, men's heads to drop off in several towns.

Follow out the fantasy of a man taking his life by instalments, instead of at one payment,—say ten years of life alternately with ten years of suspended animation.

Sentiments in a foreign language, which merely convey the sentiment without retaining to the reader any graces of style or harmony of sound, have somewhat of the charm of thoughts in one's own mind that have not yet been put into words. No possible words that we might adapt to them could realize the unshaped beauty that they appear to possess. This is the reason that translations are never satisfactory,—and less so, I should think, to one who cannot than to one who can pronounce the language.

A person to be writing a tale, and to find that it shapes itself against his intentions; that the characters act otherwise than he thought; that unforeseen events occur; and a catastrophe comes which he strives in vain to avert. It might shadow forth his own fate,—he having made himself one of the personages.

It is a singular thing, that, at the distance, say, of five feet, the work of the greatest dunce looks just as well as that of the greatest genius,—that little space being all the distance between genius and stupidity.

Mrs. Sigourney says, after Coleridge, that "poetry has been its own exceeding great reward." For the writing, perhaps; but would it be so for the reading?

Four precepts: To break off customs; to shake off spirits ill-disposed; to meditate on youth; to do nothing against one's genius.

Salem, August 31st, 1836.—A walk, yesterday, down to the shore, near the hospital. Standing on the old grassy battery, that forms a semicircle, and looking seaward. The sun not a great way above the horizon, yet so far as to give a very golden brightness, when it shone out. Clouds in the vicinity of the sun, and nearly all the rest of the sky covered with clouds in masses, not a gray uniformity of cloud. A fresh breeze blowing from land seaward. If it had been blowing from the sea, it would have raised it in heavy billows, and caused it to dash high against the rocks. But now its surface was not at all commoved with billows; there was only roughness enough to take off the gleam, and give it the aspect of iron after cooling. The clouds above added to the black appearance. A few sea-birds were flitting over the water, only visible at moments, when they turned their white bosoms towards me,—as if they were then first created. The sunshine had a singular effect. The clouds would interpose in such a manner that some objects were shaded from it, while others were strongly illuminated. Some of the islands lay in the shade, dark and gloomy, while others were bright and favored spots. The white lighthouse was sometimes very cheerfully marked. There was a schooner about a mile from the shore, at anchor, laden apparently with lumber. The sea all about her had the black, iron aspect which I have described; but the vessel herself was alight. Hull, masts, and spars were all gilded, and the rigging was made of golden threads. A small white streak of foam breaking around the bows, which were towards the wind. The shadowiness of the clouds overhead made the effect of the sunlight strange, where it fell.

September.—The elm-trees have golden branches intermingled with their green already, and so they had on the first of the month.

To picture the predicament of worldly people, if admitted to paradise.

As the architecture of a country always follows the earliest structures, American architecture should be a refinement of the log-house. The Egyptian is so of the cavern and mound; the Chinese, of the tent; the Gothic, of overarching trees; the Greek, of a cabin.

"Though we speak nonsense, God will pick out the meaning of it,"—an extempore prayer by a New England divine.

In old times it must have been much less customary than now to drink pure water. Walker emphatically mentions, among the sufferings of a clergyman's wife and family in the Great Rebellion, that they were forced to drink water, with crab-apples stamped in it to relish it.

Mr. Kirby, author of a work on the History, Habits, and Instincts of Animals, questions whether there may not be an abyss of waters within the globe, communicating with the ocean, and whether the huge animals of the Saurian tribe—great reptiles, supposed to be exclusively antediluvian, and now extinct—may not be inhabitants of it. He quotes a passage from Revelation, where the creatures under the earth are spoken of as distinct from those of the sea, and speaks of a Saurian fossil that has been found deep in the subterranean regions. He thinks, or suggests, that these may be the dragons of Scripture.

The elephant is not particularly sagacious in the wild state, but becomes so when tamed. The fox directly the contrary, and likewise the wolf.

A modern Jewish adage,—"Let a man clothe himself beneath his ability, his children according to his ability, and his wife above his ability."

It is said of the eagle, that, in however long a flight, he is never seen to clap his wings to his sides. He seems to govern his movements by the inclination of his wings and tail to the wind, as a ship is propelled by the action of the wind on her sails.

In old country-houses in England, instead of glass for windows, they used wicker, or fine strips of oak disposed checkerwise. Horn was also used. The windows of princes and great noblemen were of crystal; those of Studley Castle, Holinshed says, of beryl. There were seldom chimneys; and they cooked their meats by a fire made against an iron back in the great hall. Houses, often of gentry, were built of a heavy timber frame, filled up with lath and plaster. People slept on rough mats or straw pallets, with a round log for a pillow; seldom better beds than a mattress, with a sack of chaff for a pillow.

October 25th.—A walk yesterday through Dark Lane, and home through the village of Danvers. Landscape now wholly autumnal. Saw an elderly man laden with two dry, yellow, rustling bundles of Indian corn-stalks,—a good personification of Autumn. Another man hoeing up potatoes. Rows of white cabbages lay ripening. Fields of dry Indian corn. The grass has still considerable greenness. Wild rose-bushes devoid of leaves, with their deep, bright red seed-vessels. Meeting-house in Danvers seen at a distance, with the sun shining through the windows of its belfry. Barberry-bushes,—the leaves now of a brown red, still juicy and healthy; very few berries remaining, mostly frost-bitten and wilted. All among the yet green grass, dry stalks of weeds. The down of thistles occasionally seen flying through the sunny air.

In this dismal chamber FAME was won. (Salem, Union Street.)

Those who are very difficult in choosing wives seem as if they would take none of Nature's ready-made works, but want a woman manufactured particularly to their order.

A council of the passengers in a street: called by somebody to decide upon some points important to him.

Every individual has a place to fill in the world, and is important in some respects, whether he chooses to be so or not.

A Thanksgiving dinner. All the miserable on earth are to be invited, —as the drunkard, the bereaved parent, the ruined merchant, the broken-hearted lover, the poor widow, the old man and woman who have outlived their generation, the disappointed author, the wounded, sick, and broken soldier, the diseased person, the infidel, the man with an evil conscience, little orphan children or children of neglectful parents, shall be admitted to the table, and many others. The giver of the feast goes out to deliver his invitations. Some of the guests he meets in the streets, some he knocks for at the doors of their houses. The description must be rapid. But who must be the giver of the feast, and what his claims to preside? A man who has never found out what he is fit for, who has unsettled aims or objects in life, and whose mind gnaws him, making him the sufferer of many kinds of misery. He should meet some pious, old, sorrowful person, with more outward calamities than any other, and invite him, with a reflection that piety would make all that miserable company truly thankful.

Merry, in "merry England," does not mean mirthful; but is corrupted from an old Teutonic word signifying famous or renowned.

In an old London newspaper, 1678, there is an advertisement, among other goods at auction, of a black girl, about fifteen years old, to be sold.

We sometimes congratulate ourselves at the moment of waking from a troubled dream: it may be so the moment after death.

The race of mankind to be swept away, leaving all their cities and works. Then another human pair to be placed in the world, with native intelligence like Adam and Eve, but knowing nothing of their predecessors or of their own nature and destiny. They, perhaps, to be described as working out this knowledge by their sympathy with what they saw, and by their own feelings.

Memorials of the family of Hawthorne in the church of the village of Dundry, Somersetshire, England. The church is ancient and small, and has a prodigiously high tower of more modern date, being erected in the time of Edward IV. It serves as a landmark for an amazing extent of country.

A singular fact, that, when man is a brute, he is the most sensual and loathsome of all brutes.

A snake, taken into a man's stomach and nourished there from fifteen years to thirty-five, tormenting him most horribly. A type of envy or some other evil passion.

A sketch illustrating the imperfect compensations which time makes for its devastations on the person,—giving a wreath of laurel while it causes baldness, honors for infirmities, wealth for a broken constitution,—and at last, when a man has everything that seems desirable, death seizes him. To contrast the man who has thus reached the summit of ambition with the ambitious youth.

Walking along the track of the railroad, I observed a place where the workmen had bored a hole through the solid rock, in order to blast it; but, striking a spring of water beneath the rock, it gushed up through the hole. It looked as if the water were contained within the rock.

A Fancy Ball, in which the prominent American writers should appear, dressed in character.

A lament for life's wasted sunshine.

A new classification of society to be instituted. Instead of rich and poor, high and low, they are to be classed,—First, by their sorrows: for instance, whenever there are any, whether in fair mansion or hovel, who are mourning the loss of relations and friends, and who wear black, whether the cloth be coarse or superfine, they are to make one class. Secondly, all who have the same maladies, whether they lie under damask canopies or on straw pallets or in the wards of hospitals, they are to form one class. Thirdly, all who are guilty of the same sins, whether the world knows them or not; whether they languish in prison, looking forward to the gallows, or walk honored among men, they also form a class. Then proceed to generalize and classify the whole world together, as none can claim utter exemption from either sorrow, sin, or disease; and if they could, yet Death, like a great parent, comes and sweeps them all through one darksome portal,—all his children.

Fortune to come like a pedler with his goods,—as wreaths of laurel, diamonds, crowns; selling them, but asking for them the sacrifice of health, of integrity, perhaps of life in the battle-field, and of the real pleasures of existence. Who would buy, if the price were to be paid down?

The dying exclamation of the Emperor Augustus, "Has it not been well acted?" An essay on the misery of being always under a mask. A veil may be needful, but never a mask. Instances of people who wear masks in all classes of society, and never take them off even in the most familiar moments, though sometimes they may chance to slip aside.

The various guises under which Ruin makes his approaches to his victims: to the merchant, in the guise of a merchant offering speculations; to the young heir, a jolly companion; to the maiden, a sighing, sentimentalist lover.

What were the contents of the burden of Christian in the Pilgrim's Progress? He must have been taken for a pedler travelling with his pack.

To think, as the sun goes down, what events have happened in the course of the day,—events of ordinary occurrence: as, the clocks have struck, the dead have been buried.

24

Curious to imagine what murmurings and discontent would be excited, if any of the great so-called calamities of human beings were to be abolished,— as, for instance, death.

Trifles to one are matters of life and death to another. As, for instance, a farmer desires a brisk breeze to winnow his grain; and mariners, to blow them out of the reach of pirates.

A recluse, like myself, or a prisoner, to measure time by the progress of sunshine through his chamber.

Would it not be wiser for people to rejoice at all that they now sorrow for, and vice versa? To put on bridal garments at funerals, and mourning at weddings? For their friends to condole with them when they attained riches and honor, as only so much care added?

If in a village it were a custom to hang a funeral garland or other token of death on a house where some one had died, and there to let it remain till a death occurred elsewhere, and then to hang that same garland over the other house, it would have, methinks, a strong effect.

No fountain so small but that Heaven may be imaged in its bosom.

Fame! Some very humble persons in a town may be said to possess it,—as, the penny-post, the town-crier, the constable,—and they are known to everybody; while many richer, more intellectual, worthier persons are unknown by the majority of their fellow-citizens. Something analogous in the world at large.

The ideas of people in general are not raised higher than the roofs of the houses. All their interests extend over the earth's surface in a layer of that thickness. The meeting-house steeple reaches out of their sphere.

Nobody will use other people's experience, nor has any of his own till it is too late to use it.

Two lovers to plan the building of a pleasure-house on a certain spot of ground, but various seeming accidents prevent it. Once they find a group of miserable children there; once it is the scene where crime is plotted; at last the

25

dead body of one of the lovers or of a dear friend is found there; and, instead of a pleasure-house, they build a marble tomb. The moral,—that there is no place on earth fit for the site of a pleasure-house, because there is no spot that may not have been saddened by human grief, stained by crime, or hallowed by death. It might be three friends who plan it, instead of two lovers; and the dearest one dies.

Comfort for childless people. A married couple with ten children have been the means of bringing about ten funerals.

A blind man on a dark night carried a torch, in order that people might see him, and not run against him, and direct him how to avoid dangers.

To picture a child's (one of four or five years old) reminiscences at sunset of a long summer's day,—his first awakening, his studies, his sports, his little fits of passion, perhaps a whipping, etc.

The blind man's walk.

To picture a virtuous family, the different members examples of virtuous dispositions in their way; then introduce a vicious person, and trace out the relations that arise between him and them, and the manner in which all are affected.

A man to flatter himself with the idea that he would not be guilty of some certain wickedness,—as, for instance, to yield to the personal temptations of the Devil,—yet to find, ultimately, that he was at that very time committing that same wickedness.

What would a man do, if he were compelled to live always in the sultry heat of society, and could never bathe himself in cool solitude?

A girl's lover to be slain and buried in her flower-garden, and the earth levelled over him. That particular spot, which she happens to plant with some peculiar variety of flowers, produces them of admirable splendor, beauty, and perfume; and she delights, with an indescribable impulse, to wear them in her bosom, and scent her chamber with them. Thus the classic fantasy would be realized, of dead people transformed to flowers.

26

Objects seen by a magic-lantern reversed. A street, or other location, might be presented, where there would be opportunity to bring forward all objects of worldly interest, and thus much pleasant satire might be the result.

The Abyssinians, after dressing their hair, sleep with their heads in a forked stick, in order not to discompose it.

At the battle of Edge Hill, October 23, 1642, Captain John Smith, a soldier of note, Captain Lieutenant to Lord James Stuart's horse, with only a groom, attacked a Parliament officer, three cuirassiers, and three arquebusiers, and rescued the royal standard, which they had taken and were guarding. Was this the Virginian Smith?

Stephen Gowans supposed that the bodies of Adam and Eve were clothed in robes of light, which vanished after their sin.

Lord Chancellor Clare, towards the close of his life, went to a village church, where he might not be known, to partake of the Sacrament.

A missionary to the heathen in a great city, to describe his labors in the manner of a foreign mission.

In the tenth century, mechanism of organs so clumsy, that one in Westminster Abbey, with four hundred pipes, required twenty-six bellows and seventy stout men. First organ ever known in Europe received by King Pepin, from the Emperor Constantine, in 757. Water boiling was kept in a reservoir under the pipes; and, the keys being struck, the valves opened, and steam rushed through with noise. The secret of working them thus is now lost. Then came bellows organs, first used by Louis le Debonnaire.

After the siege of Antwerp, the children played marbles in the streets with grape and cannon shot.

A shell, in falling, buries itself in the earth, and, when it explodes, a large pit is made by the earth being blown about in all directions,— large enough, sometimes, to hold three or four cart-loads of earth. The holes are circular.

A French artillery-man being buried in his military cloak on the ramparts, a shell exploded, and unburied him.

In the Netherlands, to form hedges, young trees are interwoven into a sort of lattice-work; and, in time, they grow together at the point of junction, so that the fence is all of one piece.

To show the effect of gratified revenge. As an instance, merely, suppose a woman sues her lover for breach of promise, and gets the money by instalments, through a long series of years. At last, when the miserable victim were utterly trodden down, the triumpher would have become a very devil of evil passions,—they having overgrown his whole nature; so that a far greater evil would have come upon himself than on his victim.

Anciently, when long-buried bodies were found undecayed in the grave, a species of sanctity was attributed to them.

Some chimneys of ancient halls used to be swept by having a culverin fired up them.

At Leith, in 1711, a glass bottle was blown of the capacity of two English bushels.

The buff and blue of the Union were adopted by Fox and the Whig party in England. The Prince of Wales wore them.

In 1621, a Mr. Copinger left a certain charity, an almshouse, of which four poor persons were to partake, after the death of his eldest son and his wife. It was a tenement and yard. The parson, head-boroughs, and his five other sons were to appoint the persons. At the time specified, however, all but one of his sons were dead; and he was in such poor circumstances that he obtained the benefit of the charity for himself, as one of the four.

A town clerk arranges the publishments that are given in, according to his own judgment.

To make a story from Robert Raikes seeing dirty children at play, in the streets of London, and inquiring of a woman about them. She tells him that on Sundays, when they were not employed, they were a great deal worse, making the streets like hell; playing at church, etc. He was therefore induced to employ women at a shilling to teach them on Sundays, and thus Sunday schools were established.

To represent the different departments of the United States government by village functionaries. The War Department by watchmen, the law by constables, the merchants by a variety store, etc.

At the accession of Bloody Mary, a man, coming into a house, sounded three times with his mouth, as with a trumpet, and then made proclamation to the family. A bonfire was built, and little children were made to carry wood to it, that they might remember the circumstance in old age. Meat and drink were provided at the bonfires.

To describe a boyish combat with snowballs, and the victorious leader to have a statue of snow erected to him. A satire on ambition and fame to be made out of this idea. It might be a child's story.

Our body to be possessed by two different spirits; so that half of the visage shall express one mood, and the other half another.

An old English sea-captain desires to have a fast-sailing ship, to keep a good table, and to sail between the tropics without making land.

A rich man left by will his mansion and estate to a poor couple. They remove into it, and find there a darksome servant, whom they are forbidden by will to turn away. He becomes a torment to them; and, in the finale, he turns out to be the former master of the estate.

Two persons to be expecting some occurrence, and watching for the two principal actors in it, and to find that the occurrence is even then passing, and that they themselves are the two actors.

There is evil in every human heart, which may remain latent, perhaps, through the whole of life; but circumstances may rouse it to activity. To imagine such circumstances. A woman, tempted to be false to her husband, apparently through mere whim,—or a young man to feel an instinctive thirst for blood, and to commit murder. This appetite may be traced in the popularity of criminal trials. The appetite might be observed first in a child, and then traced upwards, manifesting itself in crimes suited to every stage of life.

The good deeds in an evil life,—the generous, noble, and excellent actions done by people habitually wicked,—to ask what is to become of them.

A satirical article might be made out of the idea of an imaginary museum, containing such articles as Aaron's rod, the petticoat of General Harrison, the pistol with which Benton shot Jackson,—and then a diorama, consisting of political or other scenes, or done in wax-work. The idea to be wrought out and extended. Perhaps it might be the museum of a deceased old man.

An article might be made respecting various kinds of ruin,—ruin as regards property,—ruin of health,—ruin of habits, as drunkenness and all kinds of debauchery,—ruin of character, while prosperous in other respects,— ruin of the soul. Ruin, perhaps, might be personified as a demon, seizing its victims by various holds.

An article on fire, on smoke. Diseases of the mind and soul,—even more common than bodily diseases.

Tarleton, of the Revolution, is said to have been one of the two handsomest men in Europe,—the Prince of Wales, afterwards George IV., being the other. Some authorities, however, have represented him as ungainly in person and rough in manners. Tarleton was originally bred to the law, but quitted law for the army early in life. He was son to a mayor of Liverpool, born in 1754, of ancient family. He wrote his own memoirs after returning from America. Afterwards in Parliament. Never afterwards distinguished in arms. Created baronet in 1818, and died childless in 1833. Thought he was not sufficiently honored among more modern heroes. Lost part of his right hand in battle of Guilford Court House. A man of pleasure in England.

It would be a good idea for a painter to paint a picture of a great actor, representing him in several different characters of one scene,— Iago and Othello, for instance.

Maine, July 5th, 1837.—Here I am, settled since night before last with B———, and living very singularly. He leads a bachelor's life in his paternal mansion, only a small part of which is occupied by a family who serve him. He provides his own breakfast and supper, and occasionally his dinner; though this is oftener, I believe, taken at the hotel, or an eating-house, or with some of his relatives. I am his guest, and my presence makes no alteration in his way of life. Our fare, thus far, has consisted of bread, butter, and cheese, crackers, herrings, boiled eggs, coffee, milk, and claret wine. He has another inmate, in the person of a queer little Frenchman, who has his breakfast, tea, and lodging here, and finds his dinner elsewhere. Monsieur S——— does not appear to be more than twenty-one years old,—a diminutive figure, with eyes askew, and otherwise of an ungainly physiognomy; he is ill-dressed also, in a coarse blue coat, thin cotton pantaloons, and unbrushed boots; altogether with as little of French coxcombry as can well be imagined, though with something of the monkey aspect inseparable from a little Frenchman. He is, nevertheless, an intelligent and well-informed man, apparently of extensive reading in his own language,—a philosopher, B——— tells me, and an infidel. His insignificant personal appearance stands in the way of his success, and prevents him from receiving the respect which is really due to his talents and acquirements; wherefore he is bitterly dissatisfied with the country and its inhabitants, and often expresses his feelings to B——— (who has gained his confidence to a certain degree) in very strong terms.

Thus here are three characters, each with something out of the common way, living together somewhat like monks. B———, our host, combines more high and admirable qualities, of that sort which make up a gentleman, than any other that I have met with. Polished, yet natural, frank, open, and straightforward, yet with a delicate feeling for the sensitiveness of his companions; of excellent temper and warm heart; well acquainted with the world, with a keen faculty of observation, which he has had many opportunities of exercising, and never varying from a code of honor and principle which is really nice and rigid in its way. There is a sort of philosophy developing itself in him which will not impossibly cause him to settle down in this or some other equally singular course of life. He seems almost to have made up his mind never to be married, which I wonder at; for he has strong affections, and is fond both of women and children.

The little Frenchman impresses me very strongly, too,—so lonely as he is here, struggling against the world, with bitter feelings in his breast, and

31

yet talking with the vivacity and gayety of his nation; making this his home from darkness to daylight, and enjoying here what little domestic comfort and confidence there is for him; and then going about all the livelong day, teaching French to blockheads who sneer at him, and returning at about ten o'clock in the evening (for I was wrong in saying he supped here,—he eats no supper) to his solitary room and bed. Before retiring, he goes to B———'s bedside, and, if he finds him awake, stands talking French, expressing his dislike of the Americans, "Je hais, je hais les Yankees!"—thus giving vent to the stifled bitterness of the whole day. In the morning I hear him getting up early, at sunrise or before, humming to himself, scuffling about his chamber with his thick boots, and at last taking his departure for a solitary ramble till breakfast. Then he comes in, cheerful and vivacious enough, eats pretty heartily, and is off again, singing French chansons as he goes down the gravel-walk. The poor fellow has nobody to sympathize with him but B———, and thus a singular connection is established between two utterly different characters.

Then here is myself, who am likewise a queer character in my way, and have come to spend a week or two with my friend of half a lifetime,—the longest space, probably, that we are ever destined to spend together; for Fate seems preparing changes for both of us. My circumstances, at least, cannot long continue as they are and have been; and B———, too, stands between high prosperity and utter ruin.

I think I should soon become strongly attached to our way of life, so independent and untroubled by the forms and restrictions of society. The house is very pleasantly situated,—half a mile distant from where the town begins to be thickly settled, and on a swell of land, with the road running at a distance of fifty yards, and a grassy tract and a gravel-walk between. Beyond the road rolls the Kennebec, here two or three hundred yards wide. Putting my head out of the window, I can see it flowing steadily along straightway between wooded banks; but arriving nearly opposite the house, there is a large and level sand island in the middle of the stream; and just below the island the current is further interrupted by the works of the mill-dam, which is perhaps half finished, yet still in so rude a state that it looks as much like the ruins of a dam destroyed by the spring freshets as like the foundations of a dam yet to be. Irishmen and Canadians toil at work on it, and the echoes of their hammering and of the voices come across the river and up to this window. Then there is a sound of the wind among the trees round the house; and, when that is silent, the calm, full, distant voice of the river becomes audible. Looking downward thither, I see the rush of the current, and mark the different eddies, with here and there white specks or streaks of foam; and often a log comes floating on, glistening in the sun, as it rolls over among the eddies, having voyaged, for aught I know, hundreds of miles from the wild upper sources of the river, passing down, down, between lines of forest, and sometimes a rough clearing, till here it floats by cultivated banks, and will soon pass by the village. Sometimes a long raft of boards comes along, requiring the nicest skill in navigating it through the narrow passage left by the mill-dam. Chaises and wagons occasionally go over the road, the riders all giving a passing glance at the dam, or perhaps alighting to examine it more fully, and at last departing with ominous shakes of the head as to the result of the enterprise. My position is so far retired from the river and mill-dam, that, though the latter is really rather a scene, yet a sort of quiet seems to be diffused over the whole. Two or three times a day this quiet is broken by the sudden thunder from a quarry, where the workmen are blasting rocks; and a peal of thunder sounds strangely in such a green, sunny, and quiet landscape, with the blue sky brightening the river.

I have not seen much of the people. There have been, however, several incidents which amused me, though scarcely worth telling. A passionate tavern-keeper, quick as a flash of gunpowder, a nervous man, and showing in his demeanor, it seems, a consciousness of his infirmity of temper. I was a witness of a scuffle of his with a drunken guest. The tavern-keeper, after they were separated, raved like a madman, and in a tone of voice having a drolly pathetic or lamentable sound mingled with its rage, as if he were lifting up his voice to weep. Then he jumped into a chaise which was standing by, whipped up the horse, and drove off rapidly, as if to give his fury vent in that way.

On the morning of the Fourth of July, two printer's apprentice-lads, nearly grown, dressed in jackets and very tight pantaloons of check, tight as their skins, so that they looked like harlequins or circus-clowns, yet appeared to think themselves in perfect propriety, with a very calm and quiet assurance of the admiration of the town. A common fellow, a carpenter, who, on the strength of political partisanship, asked B———'s assistance in cutting out great letters from play-bills in order to print "Martin Van Buren Forever" on a flag; but B——— refused. B——— seems to be considerably of a favorite with the lower orders, especially with the Irishmen and French Canadians,— the latter accosting him in the street, and asking his assistance as an interpreter in making their bargains for work.

I meant to dine at the hotel with B——— to-day; but having returned to the house, leaving him to do some business in the village, I found myself unwilling to move when the dinner-hour approached, and therefore dined very well on bread, cheese, and eggs. Nothing of much interest takes place. We live very comfortably in our bachelor establishment on a cold shoulder of mutton, with ham and smoked beef and boiled eggs; and as to drinkables, we had both claret and brown sherry on the dinner-table to-day. Last evening we had along literary and philosophical conversation with Monsieur S———. He is rather remarkably well-informed for a man of his age, and seems to have very just notions on ethics, etc., though damnably perverted as to religion. It is strange to hear philosophy of any sort from such a boyish figure. "We philosophers," he is fond of saying, to distinguish himself and his brethren from the Christians. One of his oddities is, that, while steadfastly maintaining an opinion that he is a very small and slow eater, and that we, in common with other Yankees, eat immensely and fast, he actually eats both faster and longer than we do, and devours, as B———avers, more victuals than both of us together.

Saturday, July 8th.—Yesterday afternoon, a stroll with B——— up a large brook, he fishing for trout, and I looking on. The brook runs through a valley, on one side bordered by a high and precipitous bank; on the other there is an interval, and then the bank rises upward and upward into a high hill with gorges and ravines separating one summit from another, and here and there are bare places, where the rain-streams have washed away the grass. The brook is bestrewn with stones, some bare, some partially moss-grown, and sometimes so huge as—once at least—to occupy almost the whole breadth of the current. Amongst these the stream brawls, only that this word does not express its good-natured voice, and "murmur" is too quiet. It sings along, sometimes smooth, with the pebbles visible beneath, sometimes rushing dark and swift, eddying and whitening past some rock, or underneath the hither or the farther bank; and at these places B——— cast his line, and sometimes drew out a trout, small, not more than five or six inches long. The farther we went up the brook, the wilder it grew. The opposite bank was covered with pines and hemlocks, ascending high upwards, black and solemn. One knew that there must be almost a precipice behind, yet we could not see it. At the foot you could spy, a little way within the darksome shade, the roots and branches of the trees; but soon all sight was obstructed amidst the trunks. On the hither side, at first the bank was bare, then fringed with alder-bushes, bending and dipping into the stream, which, farther on, flowed through the midst of a forest of maple, beech, and other trees, its course growing wilder and wilder as we proceeded. For a considerable distance there was a causeway, built long ago of logs, to drag lumber upon; it was now decayed and rotten, a red decay, sometimes sunken down in the midst, here and there a knotty trunk stretching across, apparently sound. The sun being now low towards the west, a pleasant gloom and brightness were diffused through the forest, spots of brightness scattered upon the branches, or thrown down in gold upon the last year's leaves among the trees. At last we came to where a dam had been built across the brook many years ago, and was now gone to ruin, so as to make the spot look more solitary and wilder than if man had never left vestiges of his toil there. It was a framework of logs with a covering of plank sufficient to obstruct the onward flow of the brook; but it found its way past the side, and came foaming and struggling along among scattered rocks. Above the dam there was a broad and deep pool, one side of which was bordered by a precipitous wall of rocks, as smooth as if hewn out and squared, and piled one upon another, above which rose the forest. On the other side there was still a gently shelving bank, and the shore was covered with tall trees, among which I particularly remarked a stately pine, wholly devoid of bark, rising white in aged and majestic ruin, thrusting out its barkless arms. It must have stood there in death many years, its own ghost. Above the dam the brook flowed through the forest, a glistening and babbling water-path, illuminated by the sun, which sent its rays almost straight along its course. It was as lovely and wild and peaceful as it could possibly have been a hundred years ago; and the traces of labors of men long departed added a deeper peace to it. I bathed in the pool, and then pursued my way down beside the brook, growing dark with a pleasant gloom, as the sun sank and the water became more shadowy. B——— says that there was formerly a tradition that the Indians used to go up this brook, and return, after a brief absence, with large masses of lead, which they sold at the trading-stations in Augusta; whence there has always been an idea that there is a lead-mine hereabouts. Great toadstools were under the trees, and some small ones as yellow and almost the size of a half-broiled yolk of an egg. Strawberries were scattered along the brookside.

Dined at the hotel or Mansion House to-day. Men were playing checkers in the parlor. The Marshal of Maine, a corpulent, jolly fellow, famed for humor. A passenger left by the stage, hiring an express onward. A bottle of champagne was quaffed at the bar.

July 9th.—Went with B——— to pay a visit to the shanties of the Irish and Canadians. He says that they sell and exchange these small houses among themselves continually. They may be built in three or four days, and are valued at four or five dollars. When the turf that is piled against the walls of some of them becomes covered with grass, it makes quite a picturesque object. It was almost dusk—just candle-lighting time—when we visited them. A young Frenchwoman, with a baby in her arms, came to the door of one of them, smiling, and looking pretty and happy. Her husband, a dark, black-haired, lively little fellow, caressed the child, laughing and singing to it; and there was a red-bearded Irishman, who likewise fondled the little brat. Then we could hear them within the hut, gabbling merrily, and could see them moving about briskly in the candlelight, through the window and open door. An old Irishwoman sat in the door of another hut, under the influence of an extra dose of rum,—she being an old lady of somewhat dissipated habits. She called to B———, and began to talk to him about her resolution not to give up her house: for it is his design to get her out of it. She is a true virago, and, though somewhat restrained by respect for him, she evinced a sturdy design to remain here through the winter, or at least for a considerable time longer. He persisting, she took her stand in the doorway of the hut, and stretched out her fist in a very Amazonian attitude. "Nobody," quoth she, "shall drive me out of this house, till my praties are out of the ground." Then would she wheedle and laugh and blarney, beginning in a rage, and ending as if she had been in jest. Meanwhile her husband stood by very quiet, occasionally trying to still her; but it is to be presumed, that, after our departure, they came to blows, it being a custom with the Irish husbands and wives to settle their disputes with blows; and it is said the woman often proves the better man. The different families also have battles, and occasionally the Irish fight with the Canadians. The latter, however, are much the more peaceable, never quarrelling among themselves, and seldom with their neighbors. They are frugal, and often go back to Canada with considerable sums of money. B——— has gained much influence both with the Irish and the French,—with the latter, by dint of speaking to them in their own language. He is the umpire in their disputes, and their adviser, and they look up to him as a protector and patron-friend. I have been struck to see with what careful integrity and wisdom he manages matters among them, hitherto having known him only as a free and gay young man. He appears perfectly to understand their general character, of which he gives no very flattering description. In these huts, less than twenty feet square, he tells me that upwards of twenty people have sometimes been lodged.

A description of a young lady who had formerly been insane, and now felt the approach of a new fit of madness. She had been out to ride, had exerted herself much, and had been very vivacious. On her return, she sat down in a thoughtful and despondent attitude, looking very sad, but one of the loveliest objects that ever were seen. The family spoke to her, but she made no answer, nor took the least notice; but still sat like a statue in her chair,—a statue of melancholy and beauty. At last they led her away to her chamber.

We went to meeting this forenoon. I saw nothing remarkable, unless a little girl in the next pew to us, three or four years old, who fell asleep, with her bead in the lap of her maid, and looked very pretty: a picture of sleeping innocence.

July 11th, Tuesday.—A drive with B——— to Hallowell, yesterday, where we dined, and afterwards to Gardiner. The most curious object in this latter place was the elegant new mansion of ———. It stands on the site of his former dwelling, which was destroyed by fire.

The new building was estimated to cost about thirty thousand dollars; but twice as much has already been expended, and a great deal more will be required to complete it. It is certainly a splendid structure; the material, granite from the vicinity. At the angles it has small, circular towers; the portal is lofty and imposing. Relatively to the general style of domestic architecture in our country, it well deserves the name of castle or palace. Its situation, too, is fine, far retired from the public road, and attainable by a winding carriage-drive; standing amid fertile fields, and with large trees in the vicinity. There is also a beautiful view from the mansion, adown the Kennebec.

Beneath some of the large trees we saw the remains of circular seats, whereupon the family used to sit before the former house was burned down. There was no one now in the vicinity of the place, save a man and a yoke of oxen; and what he was about, I did not ascertain. Mr. ——— at present resides in a small dwelling, little more than a cottage, beside the main road, not far from the gateway which gives access to his palace.

At Gardiner, on the wharf, I witnessed the starting of the steamboat New England for Boston. There was quite a collection of people, looking on or taking leave of passengers,—the steam puffing,—stages arriving, full-freighted with ladies and gentlemen. A man was one moment too late; but running along the gunwale of a mud-scow, and jumping into a skiff, he was put on board by a black fellow. The dark cabin, wherein, descending from the sunshiny deck, it was difficult to discern the furniture, looking-glasses, and mahogany wainscoting. I met two old college acquaintances, O———, who was going to Boston, and B——— with whom we afterwards drank a glass of wine at the hotel.

B———, Mons. S———, and myself continue to live in the same style as heretofore. We appear mutually to be very well pleased with each other. Mons. S——— displays many comical qualities, and manages to insure us several hearty laughs every morning and evening,—those being the seasons when we meet. I am going to take lessons from him in the pronunciation of French. Of female society I see nothing. The only petticoat that comes within our premises appertains to Nancy, the pretty, dark-eyed maid-servant of the man who lives in the other part of the house.

On the road from Hallowell to Augusta we saw little booths, in two places, erected on the roadside, where boys offered beer, apples, etc., for sale. We passed an Irishwoman with a child in her arms, and a heavy bundle, and afterwards an Irishman with a light bundle, sitting by the highway. They were husband and wife; and B——— says that an Irishman and his wife, on their journeys, do not usually walk side by side, but that the man gives the woman the heaviest burden to carry, and walks on lightly ahead!

A thought comes into my mind: Which sort of house excites the most contemptuous feelings in the beholder,—such a house as Mr.———'s, all circumstances considered, or the board-built and turf-buttressed hovels of these wild Irish, scattered about as if they had sprung up like mushrooms, in the dells and gorges, and along the banks of the river? Mushrooms, by the way, spring up where the roots of an old tree are hidden under the ground.

Thursday, July 13th.—Two small Canadian boys came to our house yesterday, with strawberries to sell. It sounds strangely to hear children bargaining in French on the borders of Yankee-land. Among other languages spoken hereabouts must be reckoned the wild Irish. Some of the laborers on the mill-dam can speak nothing else. The intermixture of foreigners sometimes gives rise to quarrels between them and the natives. As we were going to the village yesterday afternoon, we witnessed the beginning of a quarrel between a Canadian and a Yankee,—the latter accusing the former of striking his oxen. B——— thrust himself between and parted them; but they afterwards renewed their fray, and the Canadian, I believe, thrashed the Yankee soundly,—for which he had to pay twelve dollars. Yet he was but a little fellow.

Coming to the Mansion House about supper-time, we found somewhat of a concourse of people, the Governor and Council being in session on the subject of the disputed territory. The British have lately imprisoned a man who was sent to take the census; and the Mainiacs are much excited on the subject. They wish the Governor to order out the militia at once, and take possession of the territory with the strong hand. There was a British army-captain at the Mansion House; and an idea was thrown out that it would be as well to seize upon him as a hostage. I would, for the joke's sake, that it had been done. Personages at the tavern: the Governor, somewhat stared after as he walked through the bar-room; Councillors seated about, sitting on benches near the bar, or on the stoop along the front of the house; the Adjutant-General of the State; two young Blue-Noses, from Canada or the Provinces; a gentleman "thumbing his hat" for liquor, or perhaps playing off the trick of the "honest landlord" on some stranger. The decanters and wine-bottles on the move, and the beer and soda founts pouring out continual streams, with a whiz. Stage-drivers, etc., asked to drink with the aristocracy, and mine host treating and being treated. Rubicund faces; breaths odorous of brandy-and-water. Occasionally the pop of a champagne cork.

Returned home, and took a lesson in French of Mons. S———. I like him very much, and have seldom met with a more honest, simple, and apparently so well-principled a man; which good qualities I impute to his being, by the father's side, of German blood. He looks more like a German—or, as he says, like a Swiss—than a Frenchman, having very light hair and a light complexion, and not a French expression. He is a vivacious little fellow, and wonderfully excitable to mirth; and it is truly a sight to see him laugh;—every feature partakes of his movement, and even his whole body shares in it, as he rises and dances about the room. He has great variety of conversation, commensurate with his experiences in life, and sometimes will talk Spanish, ore rotundo,—sometimes imitate the Catholic priests, chanting Latin songs for the dead, in deep, gruff, awful tones, producing really a very strong impression,—then he will break out into a light, French song, perhaps of love, perhaps of war, acting it out, as if on the stage of a theatre: all this intermingled with continual fun, excited by the incidents of the passing moment. He has Frenchified all our names, calling B——— Monsieur Du Pont, myself M. de L'Aubepine, and himself M. le Berger, and all, Knights of the Round-Table. And we live in great harmony and brotherhood, as queer a life as anybody leads, and as queer a set as may be found anywhere. In his more serious intervals, he talks philosophy and deism, and preaches obedience to the law of reason and morality; which law he says (and I believe him) he has so well observed, that, notwithstanding his residence in dissolute countries, he has never yet been sinful. He wishes me, eight or nine weeks hence, to accompany him on foot to Quebec, and then to Niagara and New York. I should like it well, if my circumstances and other considerations would permit. What pleases much in Mons. S——— is the simple and childlike enjoyment he finds in trifles, and the joy with which he speaks of going back to his own country, away from the dull Yankees, who here misunderstand and despise him. Yet I have never heard him speak harshly of them. I rather think that B——— and I will be remembered by him with more pleasure than anybody else in the country; for we have sympathized with him, and treated him kindly, and like a gentleman and an equal; and he comes to us at night as to home and friends.

I went down to the river to-day to see B——— fish for salmon with a fly,—a hopeless business; for he says that only one instance has been known in the United States of salmon being taken otherwise than with a net. A few chubs were all the fruit of his piscatory efforts. But while looking at the rushing and rippling stream, I saw a great fish, some six feet long and thick in proportion, suddenly emerge at whole length, turn a somerset, and then vanish again beneath the water. It was of a glistening, yellowish brown, with its fins all spread, and looking very strange and startling, darting out so lifelike from the black water, throwing itself fully into the bright sunshine, and then lost to sight and to pursuit. I saw also a long, flat-bottomed boat go up the river, with a brisk wind, and against a strong stream. Its sails were of curious construction: a long mast, with two sails below, one on each side of the boat, and a broader one surmounting them. The sails were colored brown, and appeared like leather or skins, but were really cloth. At a distance, the vessel looked like, or at least I compared it to, a monstrous water-insect skimming along the river. If the sails had been crimson or yellow, the resemblance would have been much closer. There was a pretty spacious raised cabin in the after part of the boat. It moved along lightly, and disappeared between the woody banks. These boats have the two parallel sails attached to the same yard, and some have two sails, one surmounting the other. They trade to Waterville and thereabouts,—names, as "Paul Pry," on their sails.

      Saturday, July 15th.—Went with B——— yesterday to visit several Irish shanties, endeavoring to find out who had stolen some rails of a fence. At the first door at which we knocked (a shanty with an earthen mound heaped against the wall, two or three feet thick), the inmates were not up, though it was past eight o'clock. At last a middle-aged woman showed herself, half dressed, and completing her toilet. Threats were made of tearing down her house; for she is a lady of very indifferent morals, and sells rum. Few of these people are connected with the mill-dam,—or, at least, many are not so, but have intruded themselves into the vacant huts which were occupied by the mill-dam people last year. In two or three places hereabouts there is quite a village of these dwellings, with a clay and board chimney, or oftener an old barrel, smoked and charred with the fire. Some of their roofs are covered with sods, and appear almost subterranean. One of the little hamlets stands on both sides of a deep dell, wooded and bush-grown, with a vista, as it were, into the heart of a wood in one direction, and to the broad, sunny river in the other: there was a little rivulet, crossed by a plank, at the bottom of the dell. At two doors we saw very pretty and modest-looking young women,— one with a child in her arms. Indeed, they all have innumerable little children; and they are invariably in good health, though always dirty of face. They come to the door while their mothers are talking with the visitors, standing straight up on their bare legs, with their little plump bodies protruding, in one hand a small tin saucepan, and in the other an iron spoon, with unwashed mouths, looking as independent as any child or grown person in the land. They stare unabashed, but make no answer when spoken to. "I've no call to your fence, Misser B———." It seems strange that a man should have the right, unarmed with any legal instrument, of tearing down the dwelling-houses of a score of families, and driving the inmates forth without a shelter. Yet B——— undoubtedly has this right; and it is not a little striking to see how quietly these people contemplate the probability of his exercising it,—resolving, indeed, to burrow in their holes as long as may be, yet caring about as little for an ejectment as those who could find a tenement anywhere, and less. Yet the women, amid all the trials of their situation, appear to have kept up the distinction between virtue and vice; those who can claim the former will not associate with the latter. When the women travel with young children, they carry the baby slung at their backs, and sleeping quietly. The dresses of the new-comers are old-fashioned, making them look aged before their time.

Monsieur S—— shaving himself yesterday morning. He was in excellent spirits, and could not keep his tongue or body still, more than long enough to make two or three consecutive strokes at his beard. Then he would turn, flourishing his razor and grimacing joyously, enacting droll antics, breaking out into scraps and verses of drinking-songs, "A boire! a boire!"—then laughing heartily, and crying, "Vive la gaite!" then resuming his task, looking into the glass with grave face, on which, however, a grin would soon break out anew, and all his pranks would be repeated with variations. He turned this foolery to philosophy, by observing that mirth contributed to goodness of heart, and to make us love our fellow-creatures. Conversing with him in the evening, he affirmed, with evident belief in the truth of what he said, that he would have no objection, except that it would be a very foolish thing, to expose his whole heart, his whole inner man, to the view of the world. Not that there would not be much evil discovered there; but, as he was conscious of being in a state of mental and moral improvement, working out his progress onward, he would not shrink from such a scrutiny. This talk was introduced by his mentioning the "Minister's Black Veil," which he said he had seen translated into French, as an exercise, by a Miss Appleton of Bangor.

Saw by the river-side, late in the afternoon, one of the above-described boats going into the stream with the water rippling at the prow, from the strength of the current and of the boat's motion. By and by comes down a raft, perhaps twenty yards long, guided by two men, one at each end,—the raft itself of boards sawed at Waterville, and laden with square bundles of shingles and round bundles of clapboards. "Friend," says one man, "how is the tide now?"—this being important to the onward progress. They make fast to a tree, in order to wait for the tide to rise a little higher. It would be pleasant enough to float down the Kennebec on one of these rafts, letting the river conduct you onward at its own pace, leisurely displaying to you all the wild or ordered beauties along its banks, and perhaps running you aground in some peculiarly picturesque spot, for your longer enjoyment of it. Another object, perhaps, is a solitary man paddling himself down the river in a small canoe, the light, lonely touch of his paddle in the water making the silence seem deeper. Every few minutes a sturgeon leaps forth, sometimes behind you, so that you merely hear the splash, and, turning hastily around, see nothing but the disturbed water. Sometimes he darts straight on end out of a quiet black spot on which your eyes happen to be fixed, and, when even his tail is clear of the surface, he falls down on his side and disappears.

On the river-bank, an Irishwoman washing some clothes, surrounded by her children, whose babbling sounds pleasantly along the edge of the shore; and she also answers in a sweet, kindly, and cheerful voice, though an immoral woman, and without the certainty of bread or shelter from day to day. An Irishman sitting angling on the brink with an alder pole and a clothes-line. At frequent intervals, the scene is suddenly broken by a loud report like thunder, rolling along the banks, echoing and reverberating afar. It is a blast of rocks. Along the margin, sometimes sticks of timber made fast, either separately or several together; stones of some size, varying the pebbles and sand; a clayey spot, where a shallow brook runs into the river, not with a deep outlet, but finding its way across the bank in two or three single runlets. Looking upward into the deep glen whence it issues, you see its shady current. Elsewhere, a high acclivity, with the beach between it and the river, the ridge broken and caved away, so that the earth looks fresh and yellow, and is penetrated by the nests of birds. An old, shining tree-trunk, half in and half out of the water. An island of gravel, long and narrow, in the centre of the river. Chips, blocks of wood, slabs, and other scraps of lumber, strewed along the beach; logs drifting down. The high bank covered with various trees and shrubbery, and, in one place, two or three Irish shanties.

Thursday, July 20th.—A drive yesterday afternoon to a pond in the vicinity of Augusta, about nine miles off, to fish for white perch. Remarkables: the steering of the boat through the crooked, labyrinthine brook, into the open pond,—the man who acted as pilot,—his talking with B——— about politics, the bank, the iron money of "a king who came to reign, in Greece, over a city called Sparta,"—his advice to B——— to come amongst the laborers on the mill-dam, because it stimulated them "to see a man grinning amongst them." The man took hearty tugs at a bottle of good Scotch whiskey, and became pretty merry. The fish caught were the yellow perch, which are not esteemed for eating; the white perch, a beautiful, silvery, round-backed fish, which bites eagerly, runs about with the line while being pulled up, makes good sport for the angler, and an admirable dish; a great chub; and three horned pouts, which swallow the hook into their lowest entrails. Several dozen fish were taken in an hour or two, and then we returned to the shop where we had left our horse and wagon, the pilot very eccentric behind us. It was a small, dingy shop, dimly lighted by a single inch of candle, faintly disclosing various boxes, barrels standing on end, articles hanging from the ceiling; the proprietor at the counter, whereon appear gin and brandy, respectively contained in a tin pint-measure and an earthenware jug, with two or three tumblers beside them, out of which nearly all the party drank; some coming up to the counter frankly, others lingering in the background, waiting to be pressed, two paying for their own liquor and withdrawing. B——— treated them twice round. The pilot, after drinking his brandy, gave a history of our fishing expedition, and how many and how large fish we caught. B——— making acquaintances and renewing them, and gaining great credit for liberality and free-heartedness,—two or three boys looking on and listening to the talk,—the shopkeeper smiling behind his counter, with the tarnished tin scales beside him,—the inch of candle burning down almost to extinction. So we got into our wagon, with the fish, and drove to Robinson's tavern, almost five miles off, where we supped and passed the night. In the bar-room was a fat old countryman on a journey, and a quack doctor of the vicinity, and an Englishman with a peculiar accent. Seeing B———'s jointed and brass-mounted fishing-pole, he took it for a theodolite, and supposed that we had been on a surveying expedition. At supper, which consisted of bread, butter, cheese, cake, doughnuts, and gooseberry-pie, we were waited upon by a tall, very tall woman, young and maiden-looking, yet with a strongly outlined and determined face. Afterwards we found her to be the wife of mine host. She poured out our tea, came in when we rang the table-bell to refill our cups, and again retired. While at supper, the fat old traveller was ushered through the room into a contiguous bedroom. My own chamber, apparently the best in the house, had its walls ornamented with a small, gilt-framed, foot-square looking-glass, with a hairbrush hanging beneath it; a record of the deaths of the family written on a black tomb, in an engraving, where a father, mother, and child were represented in a graveyard, weeping over said tomb; the mourners dressed in black, country-cut clothes; the engraving executed in Vermont. There was also a wood engraving of the Declaration of Independence, with fac-similes of the autographs; a portrait of the Empress Josephine, and another of Spring. In the two closets of this chamber were mine hostess's cloak, best bonnet, and go-to-meeting apparel. There was a good bed, in which I slept tolerably well, and, rising betimes, ate breakfast, consisting of some of our own fish, and then started for Augusta. The fat old traveller had gone off with the harness of our wagon, which the hostler had put on to his horse by mistake. The tavern-keeper gave us his own harness, and started in pursuit of the old man, who was probably aware of the exchange, and well satisfied with it.

Our drive to Augusta, six or seven miles, was very pleasant, a heavy rain having fallen during the night, and laid the oppressive dust of the day before. The road lay parallel with the Kennebec, of which we occasionally had near glimpses. The country swells back from the river in hills and ridges, without any interval of level ground; and there were frequent woods, filling up the valleys or crowning the summits. The land is good, the farms look neat, and the houses comfortable. The latter are generally but of one story, but with large barns; and it was a good sign, that, while we saw no houses unfinished nor out of repair, one man at least had found it expedient to make an addition to his dwelling. At the distance of more than two miles, we had a view of white Augusta, with its steeples, and the State-House, at the farther end of the town. Observable matters along the road were the stage,—all the dust of yesterday brushed off, and no new dust contracted,—full of passengers, inside and out; among them some gentlemanly people and pretty girls, all looking fresh and unsullied, rosy, cheerful, and curious as to the face of the country, the faces of passing travellers, and the incidents of their journey; not yet damped, in the morning sunshine, by long miles of jolting over rough and hilly roads,—to compare this with their appearance at midday, and as they drive into Bangor at dusk;—two women dashing along in a wagon, and with a child, rattling pretty speedily down hill;—people looking at us from the open doors and windows;—the children staring from the wayside;—the mowers stopping, for a moment, the sway of their scythes;—the matron of a family, indistinctly seen at some distance within the house, her head and shoulders appearing through the window, drawing her handkerchief over her bosom, which had been uncovered to give the baby its breakfast,—the said baby, or its immediate predecessor, sitting at the door, turning round to creep away on all fours;—a man building a flat-bottomed boat by the roadside: he talked with B——— about the Boundary question, and swore fervently in favor of driving the British "into hell's kitchen" by main force.

Colonel B———, the engineer of the mill-dam, is now here, after about a fortnight's absence. He is a plain country squire, with a good figure, but with rather a heavy brow; a rough complexion; a gait stiff, and a general rigidity of manner, something like that of a schoolmaster. He originated in a country town, and is a self-educated man. As he walked down the gravel-path to-day, after dinner, he took up a scythe, which one of the mowers had left on the sward, and began to mow, with quite a scientific swing. On the coming of the mower, he laid it down, perhaps a little ashamed of his amusement. I was interested in this; to see a man, after twenty-five years of scientific occupation, thus trying whether his arms retained their strength and skill for the labors of his youth,— mindful of the day when he wore striped trousers, and toiled in his shirt-sleeves,—and now tasting again, for pastime, this drudgery beneath a fervid sun. He stood awhile, looking at the workmen, and then went to oversee the laborers at the mill-dam.

Monday, July, 24th.—I bathed in the river on Thursday evening, and in the brook at the old dam on Saturday and Sunday,—the former time at noon. The aspect of the solitude at noon was peculiarly impressive, there being a cloudless sunshine, no wind, no rustling of the forest-leaves, no waving of the boughs, no noise but the brawling and babbling of the stream, making its way among the stones, and pouring in a little cataract round one side of the mouldering dam. Looking up the brook, there was a long vista,— now ripples, now smooth and glassy spaces, now large rocks, almost blocking up the channel; while the trees stood upon either side, mostly straight, but here and there a branch thrusting itself out irregularly, and one tree, a pine, leaning over,— not bending,—but leaning at an angle over the brook, rough and ragged; birches, alders; the tallest of all the trees an old, dead, leafless pine, rising white and lonely, though closely surrounded by others. Along the brook, now the grass and herbage extended close to the water; now a small, sandy beach. The wall of rock before described, looking as if it had been hewn, but with irregular strokes of the workman, doing his job by rough and ponderous strength,—now chancing to hew it away smoothly and cleanly, now carelessly smiting, and making gaps, or piling on the slabs of rock, so as to leave vacant spaces. In the interstices grow brake and broad-leaved forest-grass. The trees that spring from the top of this wall have their roots pressing close to the rock, so that there is no soil between; they cling powerfully, and grasp the crag tightly with their knotty fingers. The trees on both sides are so thick, that the sight and the thoughts are almost immediately lost among confused stems, branches, and clustering green leaves,—a narrow strip of bright blue sky above, the sunshine falling lustrously down, and making the pathway of the brook luminous below. Entering among the thickets, I find the soil strewn with old leaves of preceding seasons, through which may be seen a black or dark mould; the roots of trees stretch frequently across the path; often a moss-grown brown log lies athwart, and when you set your foot down, it sinks into the decaying substance,—into the heart of oak or pine. The leafy boughs and twigs of the underbrush enlace themselves before you, so that you must stoop your head to pass under, or thrust yourself through amain, while they sweep against your face, and perhaps knock off your hat. There are rocks mossy and slippery; sometimes you stagger, with a great rustling of branches, against a clump of bushes, and into the midst of it. From end to end of all this tangled shade goes a pathway scarcely worn, for the leaves are not trodden through, yet plain enough to the eye, winding gently to avoid tree-trunks and rocks and little hillocks. In the more open ground, the aspect of a tall, fire-blackened stump, standing alone, high up on a swell of land, that rises gradually from one side of the brook, like a monument. Yesterday, I passed a group of children in this solitary valley,—two boys, I think, and two girls. One of the little girls seemed to have suffered some wrong from her companions, for she was weeping and complaining violently. Another time, I came suddenly on a small Canadian boy, who was in a hollow place, among the ruined logs of an old causeway, picking raspberries,—lonely among bushes and gorges, far up the wild valley,—and the lonelier seemed the little boy for the bright sunshine, that showed no one else in a wide space of view except him and me.

Remarkable items: the observation of Mons. S——— when B——— was saying something against the character of the French people,—"You ought not to form an unfavorable judgment of a great nation from mean fellows like me, strolling about in a foreign country." I thought it very noble thus to protest against anything discreditable in himself personally being used against the honor of his country. He is a very singular person, with an originality in all his notions;—not that nobody has ever had such before, but that he has thought them out for himself. He told me yesterday that one of his sisters was a waiting-maid in the Rocher de Cancale. He is about the sincerest man I ever knew, never pretending to feelings that are not in him,—never flattering. His feelings do not seem to be warm, though they are kindly. He is so single-minded that he cannot understand badinage, but takes it all as if meant in earnest,—a German trait. He values himself greatly on being a Frenchman, though all his most valuable qualities come from Germany. His temperament is cool and pure, and he is greatly delighted with any attentions from the ladies. A short time since, a lady gave him a bouquet of roses and pinks; he capered and danced and sang, put it in water, and carried it to his own chamber; but he brought it out for us to see and admire two or three times a day, bestowing on it all the epithets of admiration in the French language,— "Superbe! magnifique!" When some of the flowers began to fade, he made the rest, with others, into a new nosegay, and consulted us whether it would be fit to give to another lady. Contrast this French foppery with his solemn moods, when we sit in the twilight, or after B——— is abed, talking of Christianity and Deism, of ways of life, of marriage, of benevolence,—in short, of all deep matters of this world and the next. An evening or two since, he began singing all manner of English songs,—such as Mrs. Hemans's "Landing of the Pilgrims," "Auld Lang Syne," and some of Moore's,—the singing pretty fair, but in the oddest tone and accent. Occasionally he breaks out with scraps from French tragedies, which he spouts with corresponding action. He generally gets close to me in these displays of musical and histrionic talent. Once he offered to magnetize me in the manner of Monsieur P———.

Wednesday, July 26th.—Dined at Barker's yesterday. Before dinner, sat with several other persons in the stoop of the tavern. There were B———, J. A. Chandler, Clerk of the Court, a man of middle age or beyond, two or three stage people, and, near by, a negro, whom they call "the Doctor," a crafty-looking fellow, one of whose occupations is nameless. In presence of this goodly company, a man of a depressed, neglected air, a soft, simple-looking fellow, with an anxious expression, in a laborer's dress, approached and inquired for Mr. Barker. Mine host being gone to Portland, the stranger was directed to the bar-keeper, who stood at the door. The man asked where he should find one Mary Ann Russell,—a question which excited general and hardly suppressed mirth; for the said Mary Ann is one of a knot of women who were routed on Sunday evening by Barker and a constable. The man was told that the black fellow would give him all the information he wanted. The black fellow asked,—

"Do you want to see her?"

Others of the by-standers or by-sitters put various questions as to the nature of the man's business with Mary Ann. One asked,—

"Is she your daughter?"

"Why, a little nearer than that, I calkilate," said the poor devil.

Here the mirth was increased, it being evident that the woman was his wife. The man seemed too simple and obtuse to comprehend the ridicule of his situation, or to be rendered very miserable by it. Nevertheless, he made some touching points.

"A man generally places some little dependence on his wife," said he, "whether she's good or not." He meant, probably, that he rests some affection on her. He told us that she had behaved well, till committed to jail for striking a child; and I believe he was absent from home at the time, and had not seen her since. And now he was in search of her, intending, doubtless, to do his best to get her out of her troubles, and then to take her back to his home. Some advised him not to look after her; others recommended him to pay "the Doctor" aforesaid for guiding him to her; which finally "the Doctor" did, in consideration of a treat; and the fellow went off, having heard little but gibes and not one word of sympathy! I would like to have witnessed his meeting with his wife.

There was a moral picturesqueness in the contrasts of the scene,—a man moved as deeply as his nature would admit, in the midst of hardened, gibing spectators, heartless towards him. It is worth thinking over and studying out. He seemed rather hurt and pricked by the jests thrown at him, yet bore it patiently, and sometimes almost joined in the laugh, being of an easy, unenergetic temper.

Hints for characters:—Nancy, a pretty, black-eyed, intelligent servant-girl, living in Captain H————'s family. She comes daily to make the beds in our part of the house, and exchanges a good-morning with me, in a pleasant voice, and with a glance and smile,—somewhat shy, because we are not acquainted, yet capable of being made conversable. She washes once a week, and may be seen standing over her tub, with her handkerchief somewhat displaced from her white neck, because it is hot. Often she stands with her bare arms in the water, talking with Mrs. H————, or looks through the window, perhaps, at B————, or somebody else crossing the yard,—rather thoughtfully, but soon smiling or laughing. Then goeth she for a pail of water. In the afternoon, very probably, she dresses herself in silks, looking not only pretty, but lady-like, and strolls round the house, not unconscious that some gentleman may be staring at her from behind the green blinds. After supper, she walks to the village. Morning and evening, she goes a-milking. And thus passes her life, cheerfully, usefully, virtuously, with hopes, doubtless, of a husband and children.—Mrs. H———— is a particularly plump, soft-fleshed, fair-complexioned, comely woman enough, with rather a simple countenance, not nearly so piquant as Nancy's. Her walk has something of the roll or waddle of a fat woman, though it were too much to call her fat. She seems to be a sociable body, probably laughter-loving. Captain H———— himself has commanded a steamboat, and has a certain knowledge of life.

Query, in relation to the man's missing wife, how much desire and resolution of doing her duty by her husband can a wife retain, while injuring him in what is deemed the most essential point?

Observation. The effect of morning sunshine on the wet grass, on sloping and swelling land, between the spectator and the sun at some distance, as across a lawn. It diffused a dim brilliancy over the whole surface of the field. The mists, slow-rising farther off, part resting on the earth, the remainder of the column already ascending so high that you doubt whether to call it a fog or a cloud.

Friday, July 28th.—Saw my classmate and formerly intimate friend, ———, for the first time since we graduated. He has met with good success in life, in spite of circumstance, having struggled upward against bitter opposition, by the force of his own abilities, to be a member of Congress, after having been for some time the leader of his party in the State Legislature. We met like old friends, and conversed almost as freely as we used to do in college days, twelve years ago and more. He is a singular person, shrewd, crafty, insinuating, with wonderful tact, seizing on each man by his manageable point, and using him for his own purpose, often without the man's suspecting that he is made a tool of; and yet, artificial as his character would seem to be, his conversation, at least to myself, was full of natural feeling, the expression of which can hardly be mistaken, and his revelations with regard to himself had really a great deal of frankness. He spoke of his ambition, of the obstacles which he had encountered, of the means by which he had overcome them, imputing great efficacy to his personal intercourse with people, and his study of their characters; then of his course as a member of the Legislature and Speaker, and his style of speaking and its effects; of the dishonorable things which had been imputed to him, and in what manner he had repelled the charges. In short, he would seem to have opened himself very freely as to his public life. Then, as to his private affairs, he spoke of his marriage, of his wife, his children, and told me, with tears in his eyes, of the death of a dear little girl, and how it affected him, and how impossible it had been for him to believe that she was really to die. A man of the most open nature might well have been more reserved to a friend, after twelve years' separation, than

———— was to me. Nevertheless, he is really a crafty man, concealing, like a murder-secret, anything that it is not good for him to have known. He by no means feigns the good-feeling that he professes, nor is there anything affected in the frankness of his conversation; and it is this that makes him so very fascinating. There is such a quantity of truth and kindliness and warm affections, that a man's heart opens to him, in spite of himself. He deceives by truth. And not only is he crafty, but, when occasion demands, bold and fierce as a tiger, determined, and even straightforward and undisguised in his measures,—a daring fellow as well as a sly one. Yet, notwithstanding his consummate art, the general estimate of his character seems to be pretty just. Hardly anybody, probably, thinks him better than he is, and many think him worse. Nevertheless, if no overwhelming discovery of rascality be made, he will always possess influence; though I should hardly think that he would take any prominent part in Congress. As to any rascality, I rather believe that he has thought out for himself a much higher system of morality than any natural integrity would have prompted him to adopt; that he has seen the thorough advantage of morality and honesty; and the sentiment of these qualities has now got into his mind and spirit, and pretty well impregnated them. I believe him to be about as honest as the great run of the world, with something even approaching to high-mindedness. His person in some degree accords with his character,—thin and with a thin face, sharp features, sallow, a projecting brow not very high, deep-set eyes, an insinuating smile and look, when he meets you, and is about to address you. I should think that he would do away with this peculiar expression, for it reveals more of himself than can be detected in any other way, in personal intercourse with him. Upon the whole, I have quite a good liking for him, and mean to go to—to see him.

Observation. A steam-engine across the river, which almost continually during the day, and sometimes all night, may be heard puffing and panting, as if it uttered groans for being compelled to labor in the heat and sunshine, and when the world is asleep also.

Monday, July 31st.—Nothing remarkable to record. A child asleep in a young lady's arms,—a little baby, two or three months old. Whenever anything partially disturbed the child, as, for instance, when the young lady or a bystander patted its cheek or rubbed its chin, the child would smile; then all its dreams seemed to be of pleasure and happiness. At first the smile was so faint, that I doubted whether it were really a smile or no; but on further efforts, it brightened forth very decidedly. This, without opening its eyes.—A constable, a homely, good-natured, business-looking man, with a warrant against an Irishman's wife for throwing a brickbat at a fellow. He gave good advice to the Irishman about the best method of coming easiest through the affair. Finally settled,—the justice agreeing to relinquish his fees, on condition that the Irishman would pay for the mending of his old boots!

I went with Monsieur S——— yesterday to pick raspberries. He fell through an old log bridge thrown over a hollow; looking back, only his head and shoulders appeared through the rotten logs and among the bushes.—A shower coming on, the rapid running of a little barefooted boy, coming up unheard, and dashing swiftly past us, and showing the soles of his naked feet as he ran adown the path, and up the opposite rise.

Tuesday, August 1st.—There having been a heavy rain yesterday, a nest of chimney-swallows was washed down the chimney into the fireplace of one of the front rooms. My attention was drawn to them by a most obstreperous twittering; and looking behind the fireboard, there were three young birds, clinging with their feet against one of the jambs, looking at me, open-mouthed, and all clamoring together, so as quite to fill the room with the short, eager, frightened sound. The old birds, by certain signs upon the floor of the room, appeared to have fallen victims to the appetite of the cat. La belle Nancy provided a basket filled with cotton-wool, into which the poor little devils were put; and I tried to feed them with soaked bread, of which, however, they did not eat with much relish. Tom, the Irish boy, gave it as his opinion that they were not old enough to be weaned. I hung the basket out of the window, in the sunshine, and upon looking in, an hour or two after, found that two of the birds had escaped. The other I tried to feed, and sometimes, when a morsel of bread was thrust into its open mouth, it would swallow it. But it appeared to suffer very much, vociferating loudly when disturbed, and panting, in a sluggish agony, with eyes closed, or half opened, when let alone. It distressed me a good deal; and I felt relieved, though somewhat shocked when B———— put an end to its misery by squeezing its head and throwing it out of the window. They were of a slate-color, and might, I suppose, have been able to shift for themselves.—The other day a little yellow bird flew into one of the empty rooms, of which there are half a dozen on the lower floor, and could not find his way out again, flying at the glass of the windows, instead of at the door, thumping his head against the panes or against the ceiling. I drove him into the entry and chased him from end to end, endeavoring to make him fly through one of the open doors. He would fly at the circular light over the door, clinging to the casement, sometimes alighting on one of the two glass lamps, or on the cords that suspended them, uttering an affrighted and melancholy cry whenever I came near and flapped my handkerchief, and appearing quite tired and sinking into despair. At last he happened to fly low enough to pass through the door, and immediately vanished into the gladsome sunshine.—Ludicrous situation of a man, drawing his chaise down a sloping bank, to wash in the river. The chaise got the better of him, and, rushing downward as if it were possessed, compelled him to run at full speed, and drove him up to his chin into the water. A singular instance, that a chaise may run away with a man without a horse!

Saturday, August 12th.—Left Augusta a week ago this morning for ————. Nothing particular in our drive across the country. Fellow-passenger a Boston dry-goods dealer, travelling to collect bills. At many of the country shops he would get out, and show his unwelcome visage. In the tavern, prints from Scripture, varnished and on rollers,—such as the Judgment of Christ; also a droll set of colored engravings of the story of the Prodigal Son, the figures being clad in modern costume,—or, at least, that of not more than half a century ago. The father, a grave, clerical person, with a white wig and black broadcloth suit; the son, with a cocked hat and laced clothes, drinking wine out of a glass, and caressing a woman in fashionable dress. At ———— a nice, comfortable boarding-house tavern, without a bar or any sort of wines or spirits. An old lady from Boston, with her three daughters, one of whom was teaching music, and the other two schoolmistresses. A frank, free, mirthful daughter of the landlady, about twenty-four years old, between whom and myself there immediately sprang up a flirtation, which made us both feel rather melancholy when we parted on Tuesday morning.

Music in the evening, with a song by a rather pretty, fantastic little mischief of a brunette, about eighteen years old, who has married within a year, and spent the last summer in a trip to the Springs and elsewhere. Her manner of walking is by jerks, with a quiver, as if she were made of calves-feet jelly. I talk with everybody: to Mrs. T—— good sense,—to Mary, good sense, with a mixture of fun,—to Mrs. G——, sentiment, romance, and nonsense.

Walked with —— to see General Knox's old mansion,—a large, rusty-looking edifice of wood, with some grandeur in the architecture, standing on the banks of the river, close by the site of an old burial-ground, and near where an ancient fort had been erected for defence against the French and Indians. General Knox once owned a square of thirty miles in this part of the country, and he wished to settle it with a tenantry, after the fashion of English gentlemen. He would permit no edifice to be erected within a certain distance of his mansion. His patent covered, of course, the whole present town of Waldoborough and divers other flourishing commercial and country villages, and would have been of incalculable value could it have remained unbroken to the present time. But the General lived in grand style, and received throngs of visitors from foreign parts, and was obliged to part with large tracts of his possessions, till now there is little left but the ruinous mansion and the ground immediately around it. His tomb stands near the house,—a spacious receptacle, an iron door at the end of a turf-covered mound, and surmounted by an obelisk of marble. There are inscriptions to the memory of several of his family; for he had many children, all of whom are now dead, except one daughter, a widow of fifty, recently married to Hon. John H——. There is a stone fence round the monument. On the outside of this are the gravestones, and large, flat tombstones of the ancient burial-ground,—the tombstones being of red freestone, with vacant spaces, formerly inlaid with slate, on which were the inscriptions, and perhaps coats-of-arms. One of these spaces was in the shape of a heart. The people were very wrathful that the General should have laid out his grounds over this old burial-place; and he dared never throw down the gravestones, though his wife, a haughty English lady, often teased him to do so. But when the old General was dead, Lady Knox (as they called her) caused them to be prostrated, as they now lie. She was a woman of violent passions, and so proud an aristocrat, that, as long as she lived, she would never enter any house in the town except her own. When a married daughter was ill, she used to go in her carriage to the door, and send up to inquire how she did. The General was personally very popular; but his wife ruled him. The house and its vicinity, and the whole tract covered by Knox's patent, may be taken as an illustration of what must be the result of American schemes of aristocracy. It is not forty years since this house was built, and Knox was in his glory; but now the house is all in decay, while within a stone's-throw of it there is a street of smart white edifices of one and two stories, occupied chiefly by thriving mechanics, which has been laid out where Knox meant to have forests and parks. On the banks of the river, where he intended to have only one wharf for his own West Indian vessels and yacht, there are two wharves, with stores and a lime kiln. Little appertains to the mansion except the tomb and the old burial-ground, and the old fort.

The descendants are all poor, and the inheritance was merely sufficient to make a dissipated and drunken fellow of the only one of the old General's sons who survived to middle age. The man's habits were as bad as possible as long as he had any money; but when quite ruined, he reformed. The daughter, the only survivor among Knox's children (herself childless), is a mild, amiable woman, therein totally differing from her mother. Knox, when he first visited his estate, arriving in a vessel, was waited upon by a deputation of the squatters, who had resolved to resist him to the death. He received them with genial courtesy, made them dine with him aboard the vessel, and sent them back to their constituents in great love and admiration of him. He used to have a vessel running to Philadelphia, I think, and bringing him all sorts of delicacies. His way of raising money was to give a mortgage on his estate of a hundred thousand dollars at a time, and receive that nominal amount in goods, which he would immediately sell at auction for perhaps thirty thousand. He died by a chicken-bone. Near the house are the remains of a covered way, by which the French once attempted to gain admittance into the fort; but the work caved in and buried a good many of them, and the rest gave up the siege. There was recently an old inhabitant living who remembered when the people used to reside in the fort.

Owl's Head,—a watering-place, terminating a point of land, six or seven miles from Thomaston. A long island shuts out the prospect of the sea. Hither coasters and fishing-smacks run in when a storm is anticipated. Two fat landlords, both young men, with something of a contrast in their dispositions; one of them being a brisk, lively, active, jesting, fat man; the other more heavy and inert, making jests sluggishly, if at all. Aboard the steamboat, Professor Stuart of Andover, sitting on a sofa in the saloon, generally in conversation with some person, resolving their doubts on one point or another, speaking in a very audible voice; and strangers standing or sitting around to hear him, as if he were an ancient apostle or philosopher. He is a bulky man, with a large, massive face, particularly calm in its expression, and mild enough to be pleasing. When not otherwise occupied, he reads, without much notice of what is going on around him. He speaks without effort, yet thoughtfully.

We got lost in a fog the morning after leaving Owl's Head. Fired a brass cannon, rang bell, blew steam, like a whale snorting. After one of the reports of the cannon, we heard a horn blown at no great distance, the sound coming soon after the report. Doubtful whether it came from the shore or a vessel. Continued our ringing and snorting; and by and by something was seen to mingle with the fog that obscured everything beyond fifty yards from us. At first it seemed only like a denser wreath of fog; it darkened still more, till it took the aspect of sails; then the hull of a small schooner came beating down towards us, the wind laying her over towards us, so that her gunwale was almost in the water, and we could see the whole of her sloping deck.

"Schooner ahoy!" say we. "Halloo! Have you seen Boston Light this morning?"

"Yes; it bears north-northwest, two miles distant."

"Very much obliged to you," cries our captain.

So the schooner vanishes into the mist behind. We get up our steam, and soon enter the harbor, meeting vessels of every rig; and the fog, clearing away, shows a cloudy sky. Aboard, an old one-eyed sailor, who had lost one of his feet, and had walked on the stump from Eastport to Bangor, thereby making a shocking ulcer.

Penobscot Bay is full of islands, close to which the steamboat is continually passing. Some are large, with portions of forest and portions of cleared land; some are mere rocks, with a little green or none, and inhabited by sea-birds, which fly and flap about hoarsely. Their eggs may be gathered by the bushel, and are good to eat. Other islands have one house and barn on them, this sole family being lords and rulers of all the land which the sea girds. The owner of such an island must have a peculiar sense of property and lordship; he must feel more like his own master and his own man than other people can. Other islands, perhaps high, precipitous, black bluffs, are crowned with a white lighthouse, whence, as evening comes on, twinkles a star across the melancholy deep,—seen by vessels coming on the coast, seen from the mainland, seen from island to island. Darkness descending, and, looking down at the broad wake left by the wheels of the steamboat, we may see sparkles of sea-fire glittering through the gloom.

Salem, August 22d.—A walk yesterday afternoon down to the Juniper and Winter Island. Singular effect of partial sunshine, the sky being broadly and heavily clouded, and land and sea, in consequence, being generally overspread with a sombre gloom. But the sunshine, somehow or other, found its way between the interstices of the clouds, and illuminated some of the distant objects very vividly. The white sails of a ship caught it, and gleamed brilliant as sunny snow, the hull being scarcely visible, and the sea around dark; other smaller vessels too, so that they looked like heavenly-winged things, just alighting on a dismal world. Shifting their sails, perhaps, or going on another tack, they almost disappear at once in the obscure distance. Islands are seen in summer sunshine and green glory; their rocks also sunny and their beaches white; while other islands, for no apparent reason, are in deep shade, and share the gloom of the rest of the world. Sometimes part of an island is illuminated and part dark. When the sunshine falls on a very distant island, nearer ones being in shade, it seems greatly to extend the bounds of visible space, and put the horizon to a farther distance. The sea roughly rushing against the shore, and dashing against the rocks, and grating back over the sands. A boat a little way from the shore, tossing and swinging at anchor. Beach birds flitting from place to place.

59

The family seat of the Hawthornes is Wigcastle, Wigton, Wiltshire. The present head of the family, now residing there, is Hugh Hawthorne. William Hawthorne, who came over in 1635-36, was a younger brother of the family.

A young man and girl meet together, each in search of a person to be known by some particular sign. They watch and wait a great while for that person to pass. At last some casual circumstance discloses that each is the one that the other is waiting for. Moral,—that what we need for our happiness is often close at hand, if we knew but how to seek for it.

The journal of a human heart for a single day in ordinary circumstances. The lights and shadows that flit across it; its internal vicissitudes.

Distrust to be thus exemplified:—Various good and desirable things to be presented to a young man, and offered to his acceptance,—as a friend, a wife, a fortune; but he to refuse them all, suspecting that it is merely a delusion. Yet all to be real, and he to be told so, when too late.

A man tries to be happy in love; he cannot sincerely give his heart, and the affair seems all a dream. In domestic life, the same; in politics, a seeming patriot; but still he is sincere, and all seems like a theatre.

An old man, on a summer day, sits on a hill-top, or on the observatory of his house, and sees the sun's light pass from one object to another connected with the events of his past life,—as the school-house, the place where his wife lived in her maidenhood,—its setting beams falling on the churchyard.

An idle man's pleasures and occupations and thoughts during a day spent by the sea-shore: among them, that of sitting on the top of a cliff, and throwing stones at his own shadow, far below.

A blind man to set forth on a walk through ways unknown to him, and to trust to the guidance of anybody who will take the trouble; the different characters who would undertake it: some mischievous, some well-meaning, but incapable; perhaps one blind man undertakes to lead another. At last, possibly, he rejects all guidance, and blunders on by himself.

In the cabinet of the Essex Historical Society, old portraits.—Governor Leverett; a dark mustachioed face, the figure two-thirds length, clothed in a sort of frock-coat, buttoned, and a broad sword-belt girded round the waist, and fastened with a large steel buckle; the hilt of the sword steel,— altogether very striking. Sir William Pepperell, in English regimentals, coat, waistcoat, and breeches, all of red broadcloth, richly gold-embroidered; he holds a general's truncheon in his right hand, and extends the left towards the batteries erected against Louisbourg, in the country near which he is standing. Endicott, Pyncheon, and others, in scarlet robes, bands, etc. Half a dozen or more family portraits of the Olivers, some in plain dresses brown, crimson, or claret; others with gorgeous gold-embroidered waistcoats, descending almost to the knees, so as to form the most conspicuous article of dress. Ladies, with lace ruffles, the painting of which, in one of the pictures, cost five guineas. Peter Oliver, who was crazy, used to fight with these family pictures in the old Mansion House; and the face and breast of one lady bear cuts and stabs inflicted by him. Miniatures in oil, with the paint peeling off, of stern, old, yellow faces. Oliver Cromwell, apparently an old picture, half length, or one third, in an oval frame, probably painted for some New England partisan. Some pictures that had been partly obliterated by scrubbing with sand. The dresses, embroidery, laces of the Oliver family are generally better done than the faces. Governor Leverett's gloves,—the glove part of coarse leather, but round the wrist a deep, three or four inch border of spangles and silver embroidery. Old drinking-glasses, with tall stalks. A black glass bottle, stamped with the name of Philip English, with a broad bottom. The baby-linen, etc., of Governor Bradford of Plymouth County. Old manuscript sermons, some written in short-hand, others in a hand that seems learnt from print.

Nothing gives a stronger idea of old worm-eaten aristocracy—of a family being crazy with age, and of its being time that it was extinct—than these black, dusty, faded, antique-dressed portraits, such as those of the Oliver family; the identical old white wig of an ancient minister producing somewhat the impression that his very scalp, or some other portion of his personal self, would do.

The excruciating agonies which Nature inflicts on men (who break her laws) to be represented as the work of human tormentors; as the gout, by screwing the toes. Thus we might find that worse than the tortures of the Spanish Inquisition are daily suffered without exciting notice.

Suppose a married couple fondly attached to one another, and to think that they lived solely for one another; then it to be found out that they were divorced, or that they might separate if they chose. What would be its effect?

Monday, August 27th.—Went to Boston last Wednesday. Remarkables:—An author at the American Stationers' Company, slapping his hand on his manuscript, and crying, "I'm going to publish."—An excursion aboard a steamboat to Thompson's Island, to visit the Manual Labor School for boys. Aboard the steamboat several poets and various other authors; a Commodore,—Colton, a small, dark brown, sickly man, with a good deal of roughness in his address; Mr. Waterston, talking poetry and philosophy. Examination and exhibition of the boys, little tanned agriculturists. After examination, a stroll round the island, examining the products, as wheat in sheaves on the stubble-field; oats, somewhat blighted and spoiled; great pumpkins elsewhere; pastures; mowing ground;—all cultivated by the boys. Their residence, a great brick building, painted green, and standing on the summit of a rising ground, exposed to the winds of the bay. Vessels flitting past; great ships, with intricacy of rigging and various sails; schooners, sloops, with their one or two broad sheets of canvas: going on different tacks, so that the spectator might think that there was a different wind for each vessel, or that they scudded across the sea spontaneously, whither their own will led them. The farm boys remain insulated, looking at the passing show within sight of the city, yet having nothing to do with it; beholding their fellow-creatures skimming by them in winged machines, and steamboats snorting and puffing through the waves. Methinks an island would be the most desirable of all landed property, for it seems like a little world by itself; and the water may answer instead of the atmosphere that surrounds planets. The boys swinging, two together, standing up, and almost causing the rope and their bodies to stretch out horizontally. On our departure, they ranged themselves on the rails of the fence, and, being dressed in blue, looked not unlike a flock of pigeons.

On Friday, a visit to the Navy Yard at Charlestown, in company with the Naval Officer of Boston, and Cilley. Dined aboard the revenue-cutter Hamilton. A pretty cabin, finished off with bird's-eye maple and mahogany; two looking-glasses. Two officers in blue frocks, with a stripe of lace on each shoulder. Dinner, chowder, fried fish, corned beef,—claret, afterwards champagne. The waiter tells the Captain of the cutter that Captain Percival (Commander of the Navy Yard) is sitting on the deck of the anchor boy (which lies inside of the cutter), smoking his cigar. The captain sends him a glass of champagne, and inquires of the waiter what Percival says to it. "He said, sir, 'What does he send me this damned stuff for?' but drinks, nevertheless." The Captain characterizes Percival as the roughest old devil that ever was in his manners, but a kind, good-hearted man at bottom. By and by comes in the steward. "Captain Percival is coming aboard of you, sir." "Well, ask him to walk down into the cabin"; and shortly down comes old Captain Percival, a white-haired, thin-visaged, weather-worn old gentleman, in a blue, Quaker-cut coat, with tarnished lace and brass buttons, a pair of drab pantaloons, and brown waistcoat. There was an eccentric expression in his face, which seemed partly wilful, partly natural. He has not risen to his present rank in the regular line of the profession; but entered the navy as a sailing-master, and has all the roughness of that class of officers. Nevertheless, he knows how to behave and to talk like a gentleman. Sitting down, and taking in hand a glass of champagne, he began a lecture on economy, and how well it was that Uncle Sam had a broad back, being compelled to bear so many burdens as were laid on it,— alluding to the table covered with wine-bottles. Then he spoke of the fitting up of the cabin with expensive woods,—of the brooch in Captain Scott's bosom. Then he proceeded to discourse of politics, taking the opposite side to Cilley, and arguing with much pertinacity. He seems to have moulded and shaped himself to his own whims, till a sort of rough affectation has become thoroughly imbued throughout a kindly nature. He is full of antique prejudices against the modern fashions of the younger officers, their mustaches and such fripperies, and prophesies little better than disgrace in case of another war; owning that the boys would fight for their country, and die for her, but denying that there are any officers now like Hull and Stuart, whose exploits, nevertheless, he greatly depreciated, saying that the

Boxer and Enterprise fought the only equal battle which we won during the war; and that, in that action, an officer had proposed to haul down the stars and stripes, and a common sailor threatened to cut him to pieces if he should do so. He spoke of Bainbridge as a sot and a poltroon, who wanted to run from the Macedonian, pretending to take her for a line-of-battle ship; of Commodore Elliot as a liar; but praised Commodore Downes in the highest terms. Percival seems to be the very pattern of old integrity; taking as much care of Uncle Sam's interests as if all the money expended were to come out of his own pocket. This quality was displayed in his resistance to the demand of a new patent capstan for the revenue-cutter, which, however, Scott is resolved in such a sailor-like way to get, that he will probably succeed. Percival spoke to me of how his business in the yard absorbed him, especially the fitting of the Columbus seventy-four, of which ship he discoursed with great enthusiasm. He seems to have no ambition beyond his present duties, perhaps never had any; at any rate, he now passes his life with a sort of gruff contentedness, grumbling and growling, yet in good humor enough. He is conscious of his peculiarities; for when I asked him whether it would be well to make a naval officer Secretary of the Navy, he said, "God forbid, for that an old sailor was always full of prejudices and stubborn whim-whams," instancing himself; whereto I agreed. We went round the Navy Yard with Percival and Commodore Downes, the latter a sailor and a gentleman too, with rather more of the ocean than the drawing-room about him, but courteous, frank, and good-natured. We looked at ropewalks, rigging-lofts, ships in the stocks; and saw the sailors of the station laughing and sporting with great mirth and cheerfulness, which the Commodore said was much increased at sea. We returned to the wharf at Boston in the cutter's boat. Captain Scott, of the cutter, told me a singular story of what occurred during the action between the Constitution and Macedonian—he being powder-monkey aboard the former ship. A cannon-shot came through the ship's side, and a man's head was struck off, probably by a splinter, for it was done without bruising the head or body, as clean as by a razor. Well, the man was walking pretty briskly at the time of the accident; and Scott seriously affirmed that he kept walking onward at the same pace, with two jets of blood gushing from his headless trunk, till, after going about twenty feet without a head, he sunk down at once, with his legs under him.

[The corroboration of the truth of this, see Lord Bacon, Century IV. of his Sylva Sylvarum, or Natural History, in Ten Centuries, paragraph 400.]

On Saturday, I called to see E. H———, having previously appointed a meeting for the purpose of inquiring about our name. He is an old bachelor, and truly forlorn. The pride of ancestry seems to be his great hobby. He had a good many old papers in his desk at the Custom-House, which he produced and dissertated upon, and afterwards went with me to his sister's, and showed me an old book, with a record of the children of the first emigrant (who came over two hundred years ago), in his own handwriting. E———'s manners are gentlemanly, and he seems to be very well informed. At a little distance, I think, one would take him to be not much over thirty; but nearer at hand one finds him to look rather venerable,—perhaps fifty or more. He is nervous, and his hands shook while he was looking over the papers, as if he had been startled by my visit; and when we came to the crossings of streets, he darted across, cautioning me, as if both were in great danger to be run over. Nevertheless, being very quick-tempered, he would face the Devil if at all irritated. He gave a most forlorn description of his life; how, when he came to Salem, there was nobody except Mr. ——— whom he cared about seeing; how his position prevented him from accepting of civilities, because he had no home where he could return them; in short, he seemed about as miserable a being as is to be found anywhere,—lonely, and with sensitiveness to feel his loneliness, and capacities, now withered, to have enjoyed the sweets of life. I suppose he is comfortable enough when busied in his duties at the Custom-House; for when I spoke to him at my entrance, he was too much absorbed to hear me at first. As we walked, he kept telling stories of the family, which seemed to have comprised many oddities, eccentric men and women, recluses and other kinds,—one of old Philip English (a Jersey man, the name originally L'Anglais), who had been persecuted by John Hawthorne, of witch-time memory, and a violent quarrel ensued. When Philip lay on his death-bed, he consented to forgive his persecutor; "But if I get well," said he, "I'll be damned if I forgive him!" This Philip left daughters, one of whom married, I believe, the son of the persecuting John, and thus all the legitimate blood of English is in our family. E——— passed from the matters of birth, pedigree, and ancestral pride to give vent to the most arrant democracy and locofocoism that I ever happened to hear, saying that nobody ought to possess wealth longer than his own life, and that then it should return to the people, etc. He says S. I——— has a great fund of traditions about the family, which she learned from her mother or grandmother (I forget which), one of them being a Hawthorne. The old lady was a very proud woman, and, as E——— says, "proud of being proud," and so is S. I———.

October 7th.—A walk in Northfields in the afternoon. Bright sunshine and autumnal warmth, giving a sensation quite unlike the same degree of warmth in summer. Oaks,—some brown, some reddish, some still green; walnuts, yellow,—fallen leaves and acorns lying beneath; the footsteps crumple them in walking. In sunny spots beneath the trees, where green grass is overstrewn by the dry, fallen foliage, as I passed, I disturbed multitudes of grasshoppers basking in the warm sunshine; and they began to hop, hop, hop, pattering on the dry leaves like big and heavy drops of a thunder-shower. They were invisible till they hopped. Boys gathering walnuts. Passed an orchard, where two men were gathering the apples. A wagon, with barrels, stood among the trees; the men's coats flung on the fence; the apples lay in heaps, and each of the men was up in a separate tree. They conversed together in loud voices, which the air caused to ring still louder, jeering each other, boasting of their own feats in shaking down the apples. One got into the very top of his tree, and gave a long and mighty shake, and the big apples came down thump, thump, bushels hitting on the ground at once. "There! did you ever hear anything like that?" cried he. This sunny scene was pretty. A horse feeding apart, belonging to the wagon. The barberry-bushes have some red fruit on them, but they are frost-bitten. The rose-bushes have their scarlet hips.

Distant clumps of trees, now that the variegated foliage adorns them, have a phantasmagorian, an apparition-like appearance. They seem to be of some kindred to the crimson and gold cloud-islands. It would not be strange to see phantoms peeping forth from their recesses. When the sun was almost below the horizon, his rays, gilding the upper branches of a yellow walnut-tree, had an airy and beautiful effect,—the gentle contrast between the tint of the yellow in the shade and its ethereal gold in the fading sunshine. The woods that crown distant uplands were seen to great advantage in these last rays, for the sunshine perfectly marked out and distinguished every shade of color, varnishing them as it were; while the country round, both hill and plain, being in gloomy shadow, the woods looked the brighter for it.

The tide, being high, had flowed almost into the Cold Spring, so its small current hardly issued forth from the basin. As I approached, two little eels, about as long as my finger, and slender in proportion, wriggled out of the basin. They had come from the salt water. An Indian-corn field, as yet unharvested,—huge, golden pumpkins scattered among the hills of corn,—a noble-looking fruit. After the sun was down, the sky was deeply dyed with a broad sweep of gold, high towards the zenith; not flaming brightly, but of a somewhat dusky gold. A piece of water, extending towards the west, between high banks, caught the reflection, and appeared like a sheet of brighter and more glistening gold than the sky which made it bright.

Dandelions and blue flowers are still growing in sunny places. Saw in a barn a prodigious treasure of onions in their silvery coats, exhaling a penetrating perfume.

How exceeding bright looks the sunshine, casually reflected from a looking-glass into a gloomy region of the chamber, distinctly marking out the figures and colors of the paper-hangings, which are scarcely seen elsewhere. It is like the light of mind thrown on an obscure subject.

Man's finest workmanship, the closer you observe it, the more imperfections it shows; as in a piece of polished steel a microscope will discover a rough surface. Whereas, what may look coarse and rough in Nature's workmanship will show an infinitely minute perfection, the closer you look into it. The reason of the minute superiority of Nature's work over man's is, that the former works from the innermost germ, while the latter works merely superficially.

Standing in the cross-road that leads by the Mineral Spring, and looking towards an opposite shore of the lake, an ascending bank, with a douse border of trees, green, yellow, red, russet, all bright colors, brightened by the mild brilliancy of the descending sun; it was strange to recognize the sober old friends of spring and summer in this new dress. By the by, a pretty riddle or fable might be made out of the changes in apparel of the familiar trees round a house, adapted for children. But in the lake, beneath the aforesaid border of trees,—the water being, not rippled, but its glassy surface somewhat moved and shaken by the remote agitation of a breeze that was breathing on the outer lake,—this being in a sort of bay,—in the slightly agitated mirror, the variegated trees were reflected dreamily and indistinctly; a broad belt of bright and diversified colors shining in the water beneath. Sometimes the image of a tree might be almost traced; then nothing but this sweep of broken rainbow. It was like the recollection of the real scene in an observer's mind,—a confused radiance.

A whirlwind, whirling the dried leaves round in a circle, not very violently.

To well consider the characters of a family of persons in a certain condition,—in poverty, for instance,—and endeavor to judge how an altered condition would affect the character of each.

The aromatic odor of peat-smoke in the sunny autumnal air is very pleasant.

Salem, October 14th.—A walk through Beverly to Browne's Hill, and home by the iron-factory. A bright, cool afternoon. The trees, in a large part of the space through which I passed, appeared to be in their fullest glory, bright red, yellow, some of a tender green, appearing at a distance as if bedecked with new foliage, though this emerald tint was likewise the effect of frost. In some places, large tracts of ground were covered as with a scarlet cloth,— the underbrush being thus colored. The general character of these autumnal colors is not gaudy, scarcely gay; there is something too deep and rich in it: it is gorgeous and magnificent, but with a sobriety diffused. The pastures at the foot of Browne's Hill were plentifully covered with barberry-bushes, the leaves of which were reddish, and they were hung with a prodigious quantity of berries. From the summit of the hill, looking down a tract of woodland at a considerable distance, so that the interstices between the trees could not be seen, their tops presented an unbroken level, and seemed somewhat like a richly variegated carpet. The prospect from the hill is wide and interesting; but methinks it is pleasanter in the more immediate vicinity of the hill than miles away. It is agreeable to look down at the square patches of cornfield, or of potato-ground, or of cabbages still green, or of beets looking red,—all a man's farm, in short,—each portion of which he considers separately so important, while you take in the whole at a glance. Then to cast your eye over so many different establishments at once, and rapidly compare thorn,—here a house of gentility, with shady old yellow-leaved elms hanging around it; there a new little white dwelling; there an old farm-house; to see the barns and sheds and all the out-houses clustered together; to comprehend the oneness and exclusiveness and what constitutes the peculiarity of each of so many establishments, and to have in your mind a multitude of them, each of which is the most important part of the world to those who live in it,—this really enlarges the mind, and you come down the hill somewhat wiser than you go up. Pleasant to look over an orchard far below, and see the trees, each casting its own shadow; the white spires of meeting-houses; a sheet of water, partly seen among swelling lands. This Browne's Hill is a long ridge, lying in the midst of a large, level plain; it looks at a distance somewhat like a whale, with its head and tail under water, but its immense back protruding, with steep sides, and a gradual curve along its length. When you have climbed it on one side, and gaze from the summit at the other, you feel as if you had made a discovery,—the landscape being quite different on the two sides. The cellar of the house which formerly crowned the hill, and used to be named Browne's Folly, still remains, two grass-grown and shallow hollows, on the highest part of the ridge. The house consisted of two wings, each perhaps sixty feet in length, united by a middle part, in which was the entrance-hall, and which looked lengthwise along the hill. The foundation of a spacious porch may be traced on either side of the central portion; some of the stones still remain; but even where they are gone, the line of the porch is still traceable by the greener verdure. In the cellar, or rather in the two cellars, grow one or two barberry-bushes, with frost-bitten fruit; there is also yarrow with its white flower, and yellow dandelions. The cellars are still deep enough to shelter a person, all but his head at least, from the wind on the summit of the hill; but they are all grass-grown. A line of trees seems to have been planted along the ridge of the hill. The edifice must have made quite a magnificent appearance.

Characteristics during the walk:—Apple-trees with only here and there an apple on the boughs, among the thinned leaves, the relics of a gathering. In others you observe a rustling, and see the boughs shaking and hear the apples thumping down, without seeing the person who does it. Apples scattered by the wayside, some with pieces bitten out, others entire, which you pick up and taste, and find them harsh, crabbed cider-apples, though they have a pretty, waxen appearance. In sunny spots of woodland, boys in search of nuts, looking picturesque among the scarlet and golden foliage. There is something in this sunny autumnal atmosphere that gives a peculiar effect to laughter and joyous voices,—it makes them infinitely more elastic and gladsome than at other seasons. Heaps of dry leaves tossed together by the wind, as if for a couch and lounging-place for the weary traveller, while the sun is warming it for him. Golden pumpkins and squashes, heaped in the angle of a house, till they reach the lower windows. Ox-teams, laden with a rustling load of Indian corn, in the stalk and ear. When all inlet of the sea runs far up into the country, you stare to see a large schooner appear amid the rural landscape; she is unloading a cargo of wood, moist with rain or salt water that has dashed over it. Perhaps you hear the sound of an axe in the woodland; occasionally, the report of a fowling-piece. The travellers in the early part of the afternoon look warm and comfortable as if taking a summer drive; but as eve draws nearer, you meet them well wrapped in top-coats or cloaks, or rough, great surtouts, and red-nosed withal, seeming to take no great comfort, but pressing homeward. The characteristic conversation among teamsters and country squires, where the ascent of a hill causes the chaise to go at the same pace as an ox-team,—perhaps discussing the qualities of a yoke of oxen. The cold, blue aspects of sheets of water. Some of the country shops with the doors closed; others still open as in summer. I meet a wood-sawyer, with his horse and saw on his shoulders, returning from work. As night draws on, you begin to see the gleaming of fires on the ceilings in the houses which you pass. The comfortless appearance of houses at bleak and bare spots,—you wonder how there can be any enjoyment in them. I meet a girl in a chintz gown, with a small shawl on her shoulders, white stockings, and summer morocco shoes,—it looks observable. Turkeys, queer, solemn objects, in black attire, grazing about, and trying to peck the fallen apples, which slip away from their bills.

October 16th.—Spent the whole afternoon in a ramble to the seashore, near Phillips's Beach. A beautiful, warm, sunny afternoon, the very pleasantest day, probably, that there has been in the whole course of the year. People at work, harvesting, without their coats. Cocks, with their squad of hens, in the grass-fields, hunting grasshoppers, chasing them eagerly with outspread wings, appearing to take much interest in the sport, apart from the profit. Other hens picking up the ears of Indian corn. Grasshoppers, flies, and flying insects of all sorts are more abundant in these warm autumnal days than I have seen them at any other time. Yellow butterflies flutter about in the sunshine, singly, by pairs, or more, and are wafted on the gentle gales. The crickets begin to sing early in the afternoon, and sometimes a locust may be heard. In some warm spots, a pleasant buzz of many insects.

Crossed the fields near Brookhouse's villa, and came upon a long beach,— at least a mile long, I should think,—terminated by craggy rocks at either end, and backed by a high broken bank, the grassy summit of which, year by year, is continually breaking away, and precipitated to the bottom. At the foot of the bank, in some parts, is a vast number of pebbles and paving-stones, rolled up thither by the sea long ago. The beach is of a brown sand, with hardly any pebbles intermixed upon it. When the tide is part way down, there is a margin of several yards from the water's edge, along the whole mile length of the beach, which glistens like a mirror, and reflects objects, and shines bright in the sunshine, the sand being wet to that distance from the water. Above this margin the sand is not wet, and grows less and less damp the farther towards the bank you keep. In some places your footstep is perfectly implanted, showing the whole shape, and the square toe, and every nail in the heel of your boot. Elsewhere, the impression is imperfect, and even when you stamp, you cannot imprint the whole. As you tread, a dry spot flashes around your step, and grows moist as you lift your foot again. Pleasant to pass along this extensive walk, watching the surf-wave;—how sometimes it seems to make a feint of breaking, but dies away ineffectually, merely kissing the strand; then, after many such abortive efforts, it gathers itself, and forms a high wall, and rolls onward, heightening and heightening without foam at the summit of the green line, and at last throws itself fiercely on the beach, with a loud roar, the spray flying above. As you walk along, you are preceded by a flock of twenty or thirty beach birds, which are seeking, I suppose, for food on the margin of the surf, yet seem to be merely sporting, chasing the sea as it retires, and running up before the impending wave. Sometimes they let it bear them off their feet, and float lightly on its breaking summit; sometimes they flutter and seem to rest on the feathery spray. They are little birds with gray backs and snow-white breasts; their images may be seen in the wet sand almost or quite as distinctly as the reality. Their legs are long. As you draw near, they take a flight of a score of yards or more, and then recommence their dalliance with the surf-wave. You may behold their multitudinous little tracks all along your way. Before you reach the end of the beach, you become quite attached to these little sea-birds, and take much interest in their occupations. After passing in one direction, it is pleasant then to retrace your footsteps. Your tracks being all traceable, you may recall the whole mood and occupation of your mind during your first passage. Here you turned somewhat aside to pick up a shell that you saw nearer the water's edge. Here you examined a long sea-weed, and trailed its length after you for a considerable distance. Here the effect of the wide sea struck you suddenly. Here you fronted the ocean, looking at a sail, distant in the sunny blue. Here you looked at some plant on the bank. Here some vagary of mind seems to have bewildered you; for your tracks go round and round, and interchange each other without visible reason. Here you picked up pebbles and skipped them upon the water. Here you wrote names and drew faces with a razor sea-shell in the sand.

After leaving the beach, clambered over crags, all shattered and tossed about everyhow; in some parts curiously worn and hollowed out, almost into caverns. The rock, shagged with sea-weed,—in some places, a thick carpet of sea-weed laid over the pebbles, into which your foot would sink. Deep tanks among these rocks, which the sea replenishes at high tide, and then leaves the bottom all covered with various sorts of sea-plants, as if it were some sea-monster's private garden. I saw a crab in one of them; five-fingers too. From the edge of the rocks, you may look off into deep, deep water, even at low tide. Among the rocks, I found a great bird, whether a wild-goose, a loon, or an albatross, I scarcely know. It was in such a position that I almost fancied it might be asleep, and therefore drew near softly, lest it should take flight; but it was dead, and stirred not when I touched it. Sometimes a dead fish was cast up. A ledge of rocks, with a beacon upon it, looking like a monument erected to those who have perished by shipwreck. The smoked, extempore fireplace, where a party cooked their fish. About midway on the beach, a fresh-water brooklet flows towards the sea. Where it leaves the land, it is quite a rippling little current; but, in flowing across the sand, it grows shallower and more shallow, and at last is quite lost, and dies in the effort to carry its little tribute to the main.

An article to be made of telling the stories of the tiles of an old-fashioned chimney-piece to a child.

A person conscious that he was soon to die, the humor in which he would pay his last visit to familiar persons and things.

A description of the various classes of hotels and taverns, and the prominent personages in each. There should be some story connected with it,—as of a person commencing with boarding at a great hotel, and gradually, as his means grew less, descending in life, till he got below ground into a cellar.

A person to be in the possession of something as perfect as mortal man has a right to demand; he tries to make it better, and ruins it entirely.

A person to spend all his life and splendid talents in trying to achieve something naturally impossible,—as to make a conquest over Nature.

Meditations about the main gas-pipe of a great city,—if the supply were to be stopped, what would happen? How many different scenes it sheds light on? It might be made emblematical of something.

December 6th.—A fairy tale about chasing Echo to her hiding-place. Echo is the voice of a reflection in a mirror.

A house to be built over a natural spring of inflammable gas, and to be constantly illuminated therewith. What moral could be drawn from this? It is carburetted hydrogen gas, and is cooled from a soft shale or slate, which is sometimes bituminous, and contains more or less carbonate of lime. It appears in the vicinity of Lockport and Niagara Falls, and elsewhere in New

York. I believe it indicates coal. At Fredonia, the whole village is lighted by it. Elsewhere, a farm-house was lighted by it, and no other fuel used in the coldest weather.

Gnomes, or other mischievous little fiends, to be represented as burrowing in the hollow teeth of some person who has subjected himself to their power. It should be a child's story. This should be one of many modes of petty torment. They should be contrasted with beneficent fairies, who minister to the pleasures of the good.

A man will undergo great toil and hardship for ends that must be many years distant,—as wealth or fame,—but none for an end that may be close at hand,—as the joys of heaven.

Insincerity in a man's own heart must make all his enjoyments, all that concerns him, unreal; so that his whole life must seem like a merely dramatic representation. And this would be the case, even though he were surrounded by true-hearted relatives and friends.

A company of men, none of whom have anything worth hoping for on earth, yet who do not look forward to anything beyond earth!

Sorrow to be personified, and its effect on a family represented by the way in which the members of the family regard this dark-clad and sad-browed inmate.

A story to show how we are all wronged and wrongers, and avenge one another.

To personify winds of various characters.

A man living a wicked life, in one place, and simultaneously a virtuous and religious one in another.

An ornament to be worn about the person of a lady,—as a jewelled heart. After many years, it happens to be broken or unscrewed, and a poisonous odor comes out.

Lieutenant F. W——— of the navy was an inveterate duellist and an unerring shot. He had taken offence at Lieutenant F———, and endeavored to draw him into a duel, following him to the Mediterranean for that purpose, and harassing him intolerably. At last, both parties being in Massachusetts, F——— determined to fight, and applied to Lieutenant A——— to be his second. A——— examined into the merits of the quarrel, and came to the conclusion that F——— had not given F. W——— justifiable cause for driving him to a duel, and that he ought not to be shot. He instructed F——— in the use of the pistol, and, before the meeting, warned him, by all means, to get the first fire; for that, if F. W——— fired first, he, F———, was infallibly a dead man, as his antagonist could shoot to a hair's-breadth. The parties met; and F———, firing immediately on the word's being given, shot F. W——— through the heart. F. W———, with a most savage expression of countenance, fired, after the bullet had gone through his heart, and when the blood had entirely left his face, and shot away one of F———'s side-locks. His face probably looked as if he were already in the infernal regions; but afterwards it assumed an angelic calmness and repose.

A company of persons to drink a certain medicinal preparation, which would prove a poison, or the contrary, according to their different characters.

Many persons, without a consciousness of so doing, to contribute to some one end; as to a beggar's feast, made up of broken victuals from many tables; or a patch carpet, woven of shreds from innumerable garments.

Some very famous jewel or other thing, much talked of all over the world. some person to meet with it, and get possession of it in some unexpected manner, amid homely circumstances.

To poison a person or a party of persons with the sacramental wine.

A cloud in the shape of an old woman kneeling, with arms extended towards the moon.

On being transported to strange scenes, we feel as if all were unreal. This is but the perception of the true unreality of earthly things, made evident by the want of congruity between ourselves and them. By and by we become mutually adapted, and the perception is lost.

An old looking-glass. Somebody finds out the secret of making all the images that have been reflected in it pass back again across its surface.

Our Indian races having reared no monuments, like the Greeks, Romans, and Egyptians, when they have disappeared from the earth their history will appear a fable, and they misty phantoms.

A woman to sympathize with all emotions, but to have none of her own.

A portrait of a person in New England to be recognized as of the same person represented by a portrait in Old England. Having distinguished himself there, he had suddenly vanished, and had never been heard of till he was thus discovered to be identical with a distinguished man in New England.

Men of cold passions have quick eyes.

A virtuous but giddy girl to attempt to play a trick on a man. He sees what she is about, and contrives matters so that she throws herself completely into his power, and is ruined,—all in jest.

A letter, written a century or more ago, but which has never yet been unsealed.

A partially insane man to believe himself the Provincial Governor or other great official of Massachusetts. The scene might be the Province House.

A dreadful secret to be communicated to several people of various characters,—grave or gay,—and they all to become insane, according to their characters, by the influence of the secret.

Stories to be told of a certain person's appearance in public, of his having been seen in various situations, and of his making visits in private circles; but finally, on looking for this person, to come upon his old grave and mossy tombstone.

The influence of a peculiar mind, in close communion with another, to drive the latter to insanity.

To look at a beautiful girl, and picture all the lovers, in different situations, whose hearts are centred upon her.

May 11th, 1838.—At Boston last week. Items:—A young man, with a small mustache, dyed brown, reddish from its original light color. He walks with an affected gait, his arms crooked outwards, treading much on his toes. His conversation is about the theatre, where he has a season ticket,—about an amateur who lately appeared there, and about actresses, with other theatrical scandal.—In the smoking-room, two checker and backgammon boards; the landlord a great player, seemingly a stupid man, but with considerable shrewdness and knowledge of the world.—F———, the comedian, a stout, heavy-looking Englishman, of grave deportment, with no signs of wit or humor, yet aiming at both in conversation, in order to support his character. Very steady and regular in his life, and parsimonious in his disposition,—worth $ 50,000, made by his profession.—A clergyman, elderly, with a white neckcloth, very unbecoming, an unworldly manner, unacquaintance with the customs of the house, and learning them in a childlike way. A ruffle to his shirt, crimped.—A gentleman, young, handsome, and sea-flushed, belonging to Oswego, New York, but just arrived in port from the Mediterranean: he inquires of me about the troubles in Canada, which were first beginning to make a noise when he left the country,—whether they are all over. I tell him all is finished, except the hanging of the prisoners. Then we talk over the matter, and I tell him the fates of the principal men,— some banished to New South Wales, one hanged, others in prison, others, conspicuous at first, now almost forgotten.—Apartments of private families in the hotel,—what sort of domesticity there may be in them; eating in public, with no board of their own. The gas that lights the rest of the house lights them also, in the chandelier from the ceiling.— A shabby-looking man, quiet, with spectacles, at first wearing an old, coarse brown frock, then appearing in a suit of elderly black, saying nothing unless spoken to, but talking intelligently when addressed. He is an editor, and I suppose printer, of a country paper. Among the guests, he holds intercourse with gentlemen of much more respectable appearance than himself, from the same part of the country.—Bill of fare; wines printed on the back, but nobody calls for a bottle. Chairs turned down for expected guests. Three-pronged steel forks. Cold supper from nine to eleven P. M. Great, round, mahogany table, in the sitting-room, covered with papers. In the morning, before and soon after breakfast, gentlemen reading the morning papers, while others wait for their chance, or try to pick out something from the papers of yesterday or longer ago. In the forenoon, the Southern papers are brought in, and thrown damp and folded on the table. The eagerness with which those who happen to be in the room start up and make prize of them. Play-bills, printed on yellow paper, laid upon the table. Towards evening comes the Transcript.

June 15th.—The red light which the sunset at this season diffuse; there being showery afternoons, but the sun setting bright amid clouds, and diffusing its radiance over those that are scattered in masses all over the sky. It gives a rich tinge to all objects, even to those of sombre lines, yet without changing the lines. The complexions of people are exceedingly enriched by it; they look warm, and kindled with a mild fire. The whole scenery and personages acquire, methinks, a passionate character. A love-scene should be laid on such an evening. The trees and the grass have now the brightest possible green, there having been so many showers alternating with such powerful sunshine. There are roses and tulips and honeysuckles, with their sweet perfume; in short, the splendor of a more gorgeous climate than ours might be brought into the picture.

The situation of a man in the midst of a crowd, yet as completely in the power of another, life and all, as if they two were in the deepest solitude.

Tremont, Boston, June 16th.—Tremendously hot weather to-day. Went on board the Cyane to see Bridge, the purser. Took boat from the end of Long Wharf; with two boatmen who had just landed a man. Row round to the starboard side of the sloop, where we pass up the steps, and are received by Bridge, who introduces us to one of the lieutenants,—Hazard. Sailors and midshipmen scattered about,—the middies having a foul anchor, that is, an anchor with a cable twisted round it, embroidered on the collars of their jackets. The officers generally wear blue jackets with lace on the shoulders, white pantaloons, and cloth caps. Introduced into the cabin,—a handsome room, finished with mahogany, comprehending the width of the vessel; a sideboard with liquors, and above it a looking-glass; behind the cabin, an inner room, in which is seated a lady, waiting for the captain to come on board; on each side of this inner cabin, a large and convenient state-room with bed,—the doors opening into the cabin. This cabin is on a level with the quarter-deck, and is covered by the poop-deck. Going down below stairs, you come to the ward-room, a pretty large room, round which are the state-rooms of the lieutenants, the purser, surgeon, etc. A stationary table. The ship's main-mast comes down through the middle of the room, and Bridge's chair, at dinner, is planted against it. Wine and brandy produced; and Bridge calls to the Doctor to drink with him, who answers affirmatively from his state-room, and shortly after opens the door and makes his appearance. Other officers emerge from the side of the vessel, or disappear into it, in the same way. Forward of the ward-room, adjoining it, and on the same level, is the midshipmen's room, on the larboard side of the vessel, not partitioned off, so as to be shut up. On a shelf a few books; one midshipman politely invites us to walk in; another sits writing. Going farther forward, on the same level we come to the crew's department, part of which is occupied by the cooking-establishment, where all sorts of cooking is going on for the officers and men.

Through the whole of this space, ward-room and all, there is barely room to stand upright, without the hat on. The rules of the quarter-deck (which extends aft from the main-mast) are, that the midshipmen shall not presume to walk on the starboard side of it, nor the men to come upon it at all, unless to speak to an officer. The poop-deck is still more sacred,—the lieutenants being confined to the larboard side, and the captain alone having a right to the starboard. A marine was pacing the poop-deck, being the only guard that I saw stationed in the vessel,—the more stringent regulations being relaxed while she is preparing for sea. While standing on the quarter-deck, a great piping at the gangway, and the second cutter comes alongside, bringing the consul and some other gentleman to visit the vessel. After a while, we are rowed ashore with them, in the same boat. Its crew are new hands, and therefore require much instruction from the cockswain. We are seated under an awning. The guns of the Cyane are medium thirty-two pounders; some of them have percussion locks.

At the Tremont, I had Bridge to dine with me: iced champagne, claret in glass pitchers. Nothing very remarkable among the guests. A wine-merchant, French apparently, though he had arrived the day before in a bark from

Copenhagen: a somewhat corpulent gentleman, without so good manners as an American would have in the same line of life, but good-natured, sociable, and civil, complaining of the heat. He had rings on his fingers of great weight of metal, and one of them had a seal for letters; brooches at the bosom, three in a row, up and down; also a gold watch-guard, with a seal appended. Talks of the comparative price of living, of clothes, etc., here and in Europe. Tells of the prices of wines by the cask and pipe. Champagne, he says, is drunk of better quality here than where it grows.—A vendor of patent medicines, Doctor Jaques, makes acquaintance with me, and shows me his recommendatory letters in favor of himself and drugs, signed by a long list of people. He prefers, he says, booksellers to druggists as his agents, and inquired of me about them in this town. He seems to be an honest man enough, with an intelligent face, and sensible in his talk, but not a gentleman, wearing a somewhat shabby brown coat and mixed pantaloons, being ill-shaven, and apparently not well acquainted with the customs of a fashionable hotel. A simplicity about him that is likable, though, I believe, he comes from Philadelphia.—Naval officers, strolling about town, bargaining for swords and belts, and other military articles; with the tailor, to have naval buttons put on their shore-going coats, and for their pantaloons, suited to the climate of the Mediterranean. It is the almost invariable habit of officers, when going ashore or staying on shore, to divest themselves of all military or naval insignia, and appear as private citizens. At the Tremont, young gentlemen with long earlocks,—straw hats, light, or dark-mixed.—The theatre being closed, the play-bills of many nights ago are posted up against its walls.

July 4th.—A very hot, bright, sunny day; town much thronged; booths on the Common, selling gingerbread, sugar-plums, and confectionery, spruce beer, lemonade. Spirits forbidden, but probably sold stealthily. On the top of one of the booths a monkey, with a tail two or three feet long. He is fastened by a cord, which, getting tangled with the flag over the booth, he takes hold and tries to free it. He is the object of much attention from the crowd, and played with by the boys, who toss up gingerbread to him, while he nibbles and throws it down again. He reciprocates notice, of some kind or other, with all who notice him. There is a sort of gravity about him. A boy pulls his long tail, whereat he gives a slight squeak, and for the future elevates it as much as

80

possible. Looking at the same booth by and by, I find that the poor monkey has been obliged to betake himself to the top of one of the wooden joists that stick up high above. There are boys, going about with molasses candy, almost melted down in the sun. Shows: A mammoth rat; a collection of pirates, murderers, and the like, in wax. Constables in considerable number, parading about with their staves, sometimes conversing with each other, producing an effect by their presence, without having to interfere actively. One or two old salts, rather the worse for liquor: in general the people are very temperate. At evening the effect of things rather more picturesque; some of the booth-keepers knocking down the temporary structures, and putting the materials in wagons to carry away; other booths lighted up, and the lights gleaming through rents in the sail-cloth tops. The customers are rather riotous, calling loudly and whimsically for what they want; a young fellow and a girl coming arm in arm; two girls approaching the booth, and getting into conversation with the folks thereabout. Perchance a knock-down between two half-sober fellows in the crowd: a knock-down without a heavy blow, the receiver being scarcely able to keep his footing at any rate. Shoutings and hallooings, laughter, oaths,—generally a good-natured tumult; and the constables use no severity, but interfere, if at all, in a friendly sort of way. I talk with one about the way in which the day has passed, and he bears testimony to the orderliness of the crowd, but suspects one booth of selling liquor, and relates one scuffle. There is a talkative and witty seller of gingerbread holding forth to the people from his cart, making himself quite a noted character by his readiness of remark and humor, and disposing of all his wares. Late in the evening, during the fire-works, people are consulting how they are to get hone,— many having long miles to walk: a father, with wife and children, saying it will be twelve o'clock before they reach home, the children being already tired to death. The moon beautifully dark-bright, not giving so white a light as sometimes. The girls all look beautiful and fairy-like in it, not exactly distinct, nor yet dim. The different characters of female countenances during the day,—mirthful and mischievous, slyly humorous, stupid, looking genteel generally, but when they speak often betraying plebeianism by the tones of their voices. Two girls are very tired, one a pale, thin, languid-looking creature; the other plump, rosy, rather overburdened with her own little body. Gingerbread figures, in the shape of Jim Crow and other popularities.

In the old burial-ground, Charter Street, a slate gravestone, carved round the borders, to the memory of "Colonel John Hathorne, Esq.," who died in 1717. This was the witch-judge. The stone is sunk deep into the earth, and leans forward, and the grass grows very long around it; and, on account of the moss, it was rather difficult to make out the date. Other Hathornes lie buried in a range with him on either side. In a corner of the burial-ground, close under Dr. P———'s garden fence, are the most ancient stones remaining in the graveyard; moss-grown, deeply sunken. One to "Dr. John Swinnerton, Physician," in 1688; another to his wife. There, too, is the grave of Nathaniel Mather, the younger brother of Cotton, and mentioned in the Magnalia as a hard student, and of great promise. "An aged man at nineteen years," saith the gravestone. It affected me deeply, when I had cleared away the grass from the half-buried stone, and read the name. An apple-tree or two hang over these old graves, and throw down the blighted fruit on Nathaniel Mather's grave,—he blighted too. It gives strange ideas, to think how convenient to Dr. P———'s family this burial-ground is,—the monuments standing almost within arm's reach of the side windows of the parlor,—and there being a little gate from the back yard through which we step forth upon those old graves aforesaid. And the tomb of the P. family is right in front, and close to the gate. It is now filled, the last being the refugee Tory, Colonel P——— and his wife. M. P——— has trained flowers over this tomb, on account of her friendly relations with Colonel P———.

It is not, I think, the most ancient families that have tombs,—their ancestry for two or three generations having been reposited in the earth before such a luxury as a tomb was thought of. Men who founded families, and grew rich, a century or so ago, were probably the first.

There is a tomb of the Lyndes, with a slab of slate affixed to the brick masonry on one side, and carved with a coat of arms.

July 10th.—A fishing excursion, last Saturday afternoon, eight or ten miles out in the harbor. A fine wind out, which died away towards evening, and finally became quite calm. We cooked our fish on a rock named "Satan," about forty feet long and twenty broad, irregular in its shape, and of uneven surface, with pools of water here and there, left by the tide,—dark brown rock, or whitish; there was the excrement of sea-fowl scattered on it, and a few feathers. The water was deep around the rock, and swelling up and downward, waving the sea-weed. We built two fires, which, as the dusk deepened, cast a red gleam over the rock and the waves, and made the sea, on the side away from the sunset, look dismal; but by and by up came the moon, red as a house afire, and, as it rose, it grew silvery bright, and threw a line of silver across the calm sea. Beneath the moon and the horizon, the commencement of its track of brightness, there was a cone of blackness, or of very black blue. It was after nine before we finished our supper, which we ate by firelight and moonshine, and then went aboard our decked boat again,—no safe achievement in our ticklish little dory. To those remaining in the boat, we had looked very picturesque around our fires, and on the rock above them,—our statures being apparently increased to the size of the sons of Anak. The tide, now coming up, gradually dashed over the fires we had left, and so the rock again became a desert. The wind had now entirely died away, leaving the sea smooth as glass, except a quiet swell, and we could only float along, as the tide bore us, almost imperceptibly. It was as beautiful a night as ever shone,—calm, warm, bright, the moon being at full. On one side of us was Marblehead lighthouse, on the other, Baker's Island; and both, by the influence of the moonlight, had a silvery hue, unlike their ruddy beacon tinge in dark nights. They threw long reflections across the sea, like the moon. There we floated slowly with the tide till about midnight, and then, the tide turning, we fastened our vessel to a pole, which marked a rock, so as to prevent being carried back by the reflux. Some of the passengers turned in below; some stretched themselves on deck; some walked about, smoking cigars. I kept the deck all night. Once there was a little cat's-paw of a breeze, whereupon we untied ourselves from the pole; but it almost immediately died away, and we were compelled to make fast again. At about two o'clock, up rose the morning star, a round, red, fiery ball, very comparable to the moon at its rising, and, getting upward, it shone marvellously bright, and threw its long reflection into the sea, like the moon and the two lighthouses. It was Venus, and the brightest star I ever beheld; it was in the northeast. The moon made but a very small circuit in the sky, though it shone all night. The aurora borealis shot upwards to the zenith, and between two and three o'clock the first streak of dawn appeared, stretching far along the edge of the eastern horizon,— a faint streak of light; then it gradually broadened and deepened, and became a rich saffron tint, with violet above, and then an ethereal and transparent blue. The saffron became intermixed with splendor, kindling and kindling, Baker's Island lights being in the centre of the brightness, so that they were extinguished by it, or at least grew invisible. On the other side of the boat, the Marblehead lighthouse still threw out its silvery gleam, and the moon shone brightly too; and its light looked very singularly, mingling with the growing daylight. It was not like the moonshine, brightening as the evening twilight deepens; for now it threw its radiance over the landscape, the green and other tints of which were displayed by the daylight, whereas at-evening all those tints are obscured. It looked like a milder sunshine,—a dreamy sunshine,— the sunshine of a world not quite so real and material as this. All night we had heard the Marblehead clocks telling the hour. Anon, up came the sun, without any bustle, but quietly, his antecedent splendors having gilded the sea for some time before. It had been cold towards morning, but now grew warm, and gradually burning hot in the sun. A breeze sprang up, but our first use of it was to get aground on Coney Island about five o'clock, where we lay till nine or thereabout, and then floated slowly up to the wharf. The roar of distant surf, the rolling of porpoises, the passing of shoals of fish, a steamboat smoking along at a distance, were the scene on my watch. I fished during the night, and, feeling something on the line, I drew up with great eagerness and vigor. It was two of those broad-leaved sea-weeds, with stems like snakes, both rooted on a stone,—all which came up together. Often these sea-weeds root themselves on muscles. In the morning, our pilot killed a flounder with the boat-hook, the poor fish thinking himself secure on the bottom.

Ladurlad, in the Curse of Kehama, on visiting a certain celestial region, the fire in his heart and brain died away for a season, but was rekindled again on returning to earth. So may it be with me in my projected three months' seclusion from old associations.

Punishment of a miser,—to pay the drafts of his heir in his tomb.

July 13th.—A show of wax-figures, consisting almost wholly of murderers and their victims,—Gibbs and Hansley, the pirates, and the Dutch girl whom Gibbs murdered. Gibbs and Hansley were admirably done, as natural as life; and many people who had known Gibbs would not, according to the showman, be convinced that this wax-figure was not his skin stuffed. The two pirates were represented with halters round their necks, just ready to be turned off; and the sheriff stood behind them, with his watch, waiting for the moment. The clothes, halter, and Gibbs's hair were authentic. E. K. Avery and Cornell,—the former a figure in black, leaning on the back of a chair, in the attitude of a clergyman about to pray; an ugly devil, said to be a good likeness. Ellen Jewett and R. P. Robinson, she dressed richly, in extreme fashion, and very pretty; he awkward and stiff, it being difficult to stuff a figure to look like a gentleman. The showman seemed very proud of Ellen Jewett, and spoke of her somewhat as if this wax-figure were a real creation. Strong and Mrs. Whipple, who together murdered the husband of the latter. Lastly the Siamese twins. The showman is careful to call his exhibition the "Statuary." He walks to and fro before the figures, talking of the history of the persons, the moral lessons to be drawn therefrom, and especially of the excellence of the wax-work. He has for sale printed histories of the personages. He is a friendly, easy-mannered sort of a half-genteel character, whose talk has been moulded by the persons who most frequent such a show; an air of superiority of information, a moral instructor, with a great deal of real knowledge of the world. He invites his departing guests to call again and bring their friends, desiring to know whether they are pleased; telling that he had a thousand people on the 4th of July, and that they were all perfectly satisfied. He talks with the female visitors, remarking on Ellen Jewett's person and dress to them, he having "spared no expense in dressing her; and all the ladies say that a dress never set better, and he thinks he never knew a handsomer female." He goes to and fro, snuffing the candles, and now and then holding one to the face of a favorite figure. Ever and anon, hearing steps upon the staircase, he goes to admit a new visitor. The visitors,—a half-bumpkin, half country-squire-like man, who has something of a knowing air, and yet looks and listens with a good deal of simplicity and faith, smiling between whiles; a mechanic of the town; several decent-looking girls and women, who eye Ellen herself with more interest than the other figures,—women having much curiosity about such ladies; a gentlemanly sort of person, who looks somewhat ashamed of himself for being there, and glances at me knowingly, as if to intimate that he was conscious of being out of place; a boy or two, and myself, who examine wax faces and faces of flesh with equal interest. A political or other satire might be made by describing a show of wax-figures of the prominent public men; and, by the remarks of the showman and the spectators, their characters and public standing might be expressed. And the incident of Judge Tyler as related by E—— might be introduced.

A series of strange, mysterious, dreadful events to occur, wholly destructive of a person's happiness. He to impute them to various persons and causes, but ultimately finds that he is himself the sole agent. Moral, that our welfare depends on ourselves.

The strange incident in the court of Charles IX. of France: he and five other maskers being attired in coats of linen covered with pitch and bestuck with flax to represent hairy savages. They entered the hall dancing, the five being fastened together, and the king in front. By accident the five were set on fire with a torch. Two were burned to death on the spot, two afterwards died; one fled to the buttery, and jumped into a vessel of water. It might be represented as the fate of a squad of dissolute men.

A perception, for a moment, of one's eventual and moral self, as if it were another person,—the observant faculty being separated, and looking intently at the qualities of the character. There is a surprise when this happens,—this getting out of one's self,—and then the observer sees how queer a fellow he is.

July 27th.—Left home [Salem] on the 23d instant. To Boston by stage, and took the afternoon cars for Worcester. A little boy returning from the city, several miles, with a basket of empty custard-cups, the contents of which he had probably sold at the depot. Stopped at the Temperance House. An old gentleman, Mr. Phillips of Boston, got into conversation with one, and inquired very freely as to my character, tastes, habits, and circumstances,—a freedom sanctioned by his age, his kindly and beneficent spirit, and the wisdom of his advice. It is strange how little impertinence depends on what is actually said, but rather on the manner and motives of saying it. "I want to do you good," said he with warmth, after becoming, apparently, moved by my communications. "Well, sir," replied I, "I wish you could, for both our sakes; for I have no doubt it will be a great satisfaction to you." He asked the most direct questions of another young man; for instance, "Are you married?" having before ascertained that point with regard to myself. He told me by all means to act, in whatever way; observing that he himself would have no objection to be a servant, if no other mode of action presented itself.

The landlord of the tavern, a decent, active, grave, attentive personage, giving me several cards of his house to distribute on my departure. A judge, a stout, hearty country squire, looking elderly; a hale and rugged man, in a black coat, and thin, light pantaloons.

Started for Northampton at half past nine in the morning. A respectable sort of man and his son on their way to Niagara,—grocers, I believe, and calculating how to perform the tour, subtracting as few days as possible from the shop. Somewhat inexperienced travellers, and comparing everything advantageously or otherwise with Boston customs; and considering themselves a long way from home, while yet short of a hundred miles from it. Two ladies, rather good-looking. I rode outside nearly all day, and was very sociable with the driver and another outside passenger. Towards night, took up an essence-vendor for a short distance. He was returning home, after having been out on a tour two or three weeks; and nearly exhausted his stock. He was not exclusively an essence-pedler, having a large tin box, which had been filled with dry goods, combs, jewelry, etc., now mostly sold out. His essences were of anise-seed, cloves, red-cedar, wormwood, together with opodeldoc, and an oil for the hair. These matters are concocted at Ashfield, and the pedlers are sent about with vast quantities. Cologne-water is among the essences manufactured, though the bottles have foreign labels on them. The pedler was good-natured and communicative, and spoke very frankly about his trade, which he seemed to like better than farming, though his experience of it is yet brief. He spoke of the trials of temper to which pedlers are subjected, but said that it was necessary to be forbearing, because the same road must be travelled again and again. The pedlers find satisfaction for all contumelies in making good bargains out of their customers. This man was a pedler in quite a small way, making but a narrow circuit, and carrying no more than an open basket full of essences; but some go out with wagon-loads. He himself contemplated a trip westward, in which case he would send on quantities of his wares ahead to different stations. He seemed to enjoy the intercourse and seeing of the world. He pointed out a rough place in the road, where his stock of essences had formerly been broken by a jolt of the stage. What a waste of sweet smells on the desert air! The essence-labels stated the efficacy of the stuffs for various complaints of children and grown people. The driver was an acquaintance of the pedler, and so gave him his drive for nothing, though the pedler pretended to wish to force some silver into his hand; and afterwards he got down to water the horses, while the driver was busied with other matters. This driver was a little, dark ragamuffin, apparently of irascible temper, speaking with great disapprobation of his way-bill not being timed accurately, but so as to make it appear as if he were longer upon the road than he was. As he spoke, the blood darkened in his cheek, and his eye looked ominous and angry, as if he were enraged with the person to whom he was speaking; yet he had not real grit, for he had never said a word of his grievances to those concerned. "I mean to tell them of it by and by. I won't bear it more than three or four times more," said he.

Left Northampton the next morning, between one and two o'clock. Three other passengers, whose faces were not visible for some hours; so we went on through unknown space, saying nothing, glancing forth sometimes to see the gleam of the lanterns on wayside objects.

How very desolate looks a forest when seen in this way,—as if, should you venture one step within its wild, tangled, many-stemmed, and dark-shadowed verge, you would inevitably be lost forever. Sometimes we passed a house, or rumbled through a village, stopping perhaps to arouse some drowsy postmaster, who appeared at the door in shirt and pantaloons, yawning, received the mail, returned it again, and was yawning when last seen. A few words exchanged among the passengers, as they roused themselves from their half-slumbers, or dreamy, slumber-like abstraction. Meantime dawn broke, our faces became partially visible, the morning air grew colder, and finally cloudy day came on. We found ourselves driving through quite a romantic country, with hills or mountains on all sides, a stream on one side, bordered by a high, precipitous bank, up which would have grown pines, only that, losing their footholds, many of them had slipped downward. The road was not the safest in the world; for often the carriage approached within two or three feet of a precipice; but the driver, a merry fellow, lolled on his box, with his feet protruding horizontally, and rattled on at the rate of ten miles an hour. Breakfast between four and five,—newly caught trout, salmon, ham, boiled eggs, and other niceties,—truly excellent. A bunch of pickerel, intended for a tavern-keeper farther on, was carried by the stage-driver. The drivers carry a "time-watch" enclosed in a small wooden case, with a lock, so that it may be known in what time they perform their stages. They are allowed so many hours and minutes to do their work, and their desire to go as fast as possible, combined with that of keeping their horses in good order, produces about a right medium.

One of the passengers was a young man who had been in Pennsylvania, keeping a school,—a genteel enough young man, but not a gentleman. He took neither supper nor breakfast, excusing himself from one as being weary with riding all day, and from the other because it was so early. He attacked me for a subscription for "building up a destitute church," of which he had taken an agency, and had collected two or three hundred dollars, but wanted as many thousands. Betimes in the morning, on the descent of a mountain, we arrived at a house where dwelt the married sister of the young man, whom he was going to visit.

He alighted, saw his trunk taken off, and then, having perceived his sister at the door, and turning to bid us farewell, there was a broad smile, even a laugh of pleasure, which did him more credit with me than anything else; for hitherto there had been a disagreeable scornful twist upon his face, perhaps, however, merely superficial. I saw, as the stage drove off, his comely sister approaching with a lighted-up face to greet him, and one passenger on the front seat beheld them meet. "Is it an affectionate greeting?" inquired I. "Yes," said he, "I should like to share it"; whereby I concluded that there was a kiss exchanged.

The highest point of our journey was at Windsor, where we could see leagues around over the mountain, a terribly bare, bleak spot, fit for nothing but sheep, and without shelter of woods. We rattled downward into a warmer region, beholding as we went the sun shining on portions of the landscape, miles ahead of us, while we were yet in chillness and gloom. It is probable that during a part of the stage the mists around us looked like sky clouds to those in the lower regions. Think of driving a stage-coach through the clouds! Seasonably in the forenoon we arrived at Pittsfield.

Pittsfield is a large village, quite shut in by mountain walls, generally extending like a rampart on all sides of it, but with insulated great hills rising here and there in the outline. The area of the town is level; its houses are handsome, mostly wooden and white; but some are of brick, painted deep red, the bricks being not of a healthy, natural color. There are handsome churches, Gothic and others, and a court-house and an academy; the court-house having a marble front. There is a small wall in the centre of the town, and in the centre of the Mall rises an elm of the loftiest and straightest stem that ever I beheld, without a branch or leaf upon it till it has soared seventy or perhaps a hundred feet into the air. The top branches unfortunately have been shattered somehow or other, so that it does not cast a broad shade; probably they were broken by their own ponderous foliage. The central square of Pittsfield presents all the bustle of a thriving village,—the farmers of the vicinity in light wagons, sulkies, or on horseback; stages at the door of the Berkshire Hotel, under the stoop of which sit or lounge the guests, stage-people, and idlers, observing or assisting in the arrivals and departures. Huge trunks and bandboxes unladed and laded. The courtesy shown to ladies in aiding them to alight, in a shower, under umbrellas. The dull looks of passengers, who have driven all night, scarcely brightened by the excitement of arriving at a new place. The stage agent demanding the names of those who are going on,—some to Lebanon Springs, some to Albany. The toddy-stick is still busy at these Berkshire public-houses. At dinner soup preliminary, in city style. Guests: the court people; Briggs, member of Congress, attending a trial here; horse-dealers, country squires, store-keepers in the village, etc. My room, a narrow crib overlooking a back court-yard, where a young man and a lad were drawing water for the maid-servants,—their jokes, especially those of the lad, of whose wit the elder fellow, being a blockhead himself, was in great admiration, and declared to another that he knew as much as them both. Yet he was not very witty. Once in a while the maid-servants would come to the door, and hear and respond to their jokes, with a kind of restraint, yet both permitting and enjoying them.

After or about sunset there was a heavy shower, the thunder rumbling round and round the mountain wall, and the clouds stretching from rampart to rampart. When it abated, the clouds in all parts of the visible heavens were tinged with glory from the west; some that hung low being purple and gold, while the higher ones were gray. The slender curve of the new moon was also visible brightening amidst the fading brightness of the sunny part of the sky. There are marble-quarries in and near Pittsfield, which accounts for the fact that there are none but marble gravestones in the burial-grounds; some of the monuments well carved; but the marble does not withstand the wear and tear of time and weather so well as the imported marble, and the sculpture soon loses its sharp outline. The door of one tomb, a wooden door, opening in the side of a green mound, surmounted by a marble obelisk, having been shaken from its hinges by the late explosion of the powder-house, and incompletely repaired, I peeped in at the crevices, and saw the coffins. It was the tomb of Rev. Thomas Allen, first minister of Pittsfield, deceased in 1810. It contained three coffins, all with white mould on their tops: one, a small child's, rested upon another, and the other was on the opposite side of the tomb, and the lid was considerably displaced; but, the tomb being dark, I could see neither corpse nor skeleton.

Marble also occurs here in North Adams, and thus some very ordinary houses have marble doorsteps, and even the stone walls are built of fragments of marble.

Wednesday, 26th.—Left Pittsfield at about eight o'clock in the Bennington stage, intending to go to Williamstown. Inside passengers,—a new-married couple taking a jaunt. The lady, with a clear, pale complexion, and a rather pensive cast of countenance, slender, and with a genteel figure; the bridegroom, a shopkeeper in New York probably, a young man with a stout black beard, black eyebrows, which formed one line across his forehead. They were very loving; and while the stage stopped, I watched them, quite entranced in each other, both leaning sideways against the back of the coach, and perusing their mutual comeliness, and apparently making complimentary observations upon it to one another. The bride appeared the most absorbed and devoted, referring her whole being to him. The gentleman seemed in a most paradisiacal mood, smiling ineffably upon his bride, and, when she spoke, responding to her with a benign expression of matrimonial sweetness, and, as it were, compassion for the "weaker vessel," mingled with great love and pleasant humor. It was very droll. The driver peeped into the coach once, and said that he had his arm round her waist. He took little freedoms with her, tapping her with his cane,—love-pats; and she seemed to see nothing amiss. They kept eating gingerbread all along the road, and dined heartily notwithstanding.

Our driver was a slender, lathe-like, round-backed, rough-bearded, thin-visaged, middle-aged Yankee, who became very communicative during our drive. He was not bred a stage-driver, but had undertaken the business temporarily, as a favor to his brother-in-law. He was a native of these Berkshire mountains, but had formerly emigrated to Ohio, and had returned for a time to try the benefit of her native air on his wife's declining health,—she having complaints of a consumptive nature. He pointed out the house where he was married to her, and told the name of the country squire who tied the knot. His wife has little or no chance of recovery, and he said he would never marry again,—this resolution being expressed in answer to a remark of mine relative to a second marriage. He has no children. I pointed to a hill at some distance before us, and asked what it was. "That, sir," said he, "is a very high hill. It is known by the name of Graylock." He seemed to feel that this was a more poetical epithet than Saddleback, which is a more usual name for it. Graylock, or Saddleback, is quite a respectable mountain; and I suppose the former name has been given to it because it often has a gray cloud, or lock of gray mist, upon its head. It does not ascend into a peak, but heaves up a round ball, and has supporting ridges on each side. Its summit is not bare, like that of Mount Washington, but covered with forests. The driver said, that several years since the students of Williams College erected a building for an observatory on the top of the mountain, and employed him to haul the materials for constructing it; and he was the only man who had driven an ox-team up Graylock. It was necessary to drive the team round and round, in ascending. President Griffin rode up on horseback.

Along our road we passed villages, and often factories, the machinery whirring, and girls looking out of the windows at the stage, with heads averted from their tasks, but still busy. These factories have two, three, or more boarding-houses near them, two stories high, and of double length,—often with bean-vines running up round the doors, and with altogether a domestic look. There are several factories in different parts of North Adams, along the banks of a stream,—a wild, highland rivulet, which, however, does vast work of a civilized nature. It is strange to see such a rough and untamed stream as it looks to be so subdued to the purposes of man, and making cottons and woollens, sawing boards and marbles, and giving employment to so many men and girls. And there is a sort of picturesqueness in finding these factories, supremely artificial establishments, in the midst of such wild scenery. For now the stream will be flowing through a rude forest, with the trees erect and dark, as when the Indians fished there; and it brawls and tumbles and eddies over its rock-strewn current. Perhaps there is a precipice, hundreds of feet high, beside it, down which, by heavy rains or the melting of snows, great pine-trees have slid or fallen headlong, and lie at the bottom, or half-way down, while their brethren seem to be gazing at their fall from the summit, and anticipating a like fate. And then, taking a turn in the road, behold these factories and their range of boarding-houses, with the girls looking out of the windows as aforesaid! And perhaps the wild scenery is all around the very site of the factory, and mingles its impression strangely with those opposite ones. These observations were made during a walk yesterday.

I bathed in a pool of the stream that was out of sight, and where its brawling waters were deep enough to cover me, when I lay at length. A part of the road along which I walked was on the edge of a precipice, falling down straight towards the stream; and in one place the passage of heavy loads had sunk it, so that soon, probably, there will be an avalanche, perhaps carrying a stage-coach or heavy wagon down into the bed of the river.

I met occasional wayfarers; once two women in a cart,—decent, brown-visaged, country matrons,—and then an apparent doctor, of whom there are seven or thereabouts in North Adams; for though this vicinity is very healthy, yet the physicians are obliged to ride considerable distances among the mountain towns, and their practice is very laborious. A nod is always exchanged between strangers meeting on the road. This morning an underwitted old man met me on a walk, and held a pretty long conversation, insisting upon shaking hands (to which I was averse, lest his band should not be clean), and insisting on his right to do so, as being "a friend of mankind." He was a gray, bald-headed, wrinkled-visaged figure, decently dressed, with cowhide shoes, a coat on one arm, and an umbrella on the other, and said that he was going to see a widow in the neighborhood. Finding that I was not provided with a wife, he recommended a certain maiden of forty years, who had three hundred acres of land. He spoke of his children, who are proprietors of a circus establishment, and have taken a granddaughter to bring up in their way of life; and he gave me a message to tell them in case we should meet. While this old man is wandering among the hills, his children are the gaze of multitudes. He told me the place where he was born, directing me to it by pointing to a wreath of mist which lay on the side of a mountain ridge, which he termed "the smoke yonder." Speaking of the widow, he said: "My wife has been dead these seven years, and why should not I enjoy myself a little?" His manner was full of quirks and quips and eccentricities, waving his umbrella and gesticulating strangely, with a great deal of action. I suppose, to help his natural foolishness, he had been drinking. We parted, he exhorting me not to forget his message to his sons, and I shouting after him a request to be remembered to the widow. Conceive something tragical to be talked about, and much might be made of this interview in a wild road among the hills, with Graylock, at a great distance, looking sombre and angry, by reason of the gray, heavy mist upon his head.

The morning was cloudy, and all the near landscape lay unsunned; but there was sunshine on distant tracts, in the valleys, and in specks upon the mountain-tops. Between the ridges of hills, there are long, wide, deep valleys, extending for miles and miles, with houses scattered along them. A bulky company of mountains, swelling round head over round head, rises insulated by such broad vales from the surrounding ridges.

I ought to have mentioned that I arrived at North Adams in the forenoon of the 26th, and, liking the aspect of matters indifferently well, determined to make my headquarters here for a short time.

On the road to Northampton, we passed a tame crow, which was sitting on the peak of a barn. The crow flew down from its perch, and followed us a great distance, hopping along the road, and flying, with its large, black, flapping wings, from post to post of the fence, or from tree to tree. At last he gave up the pursuit with a croak of disappointment. The driver said, perhaps correctly, that the crow had scented some salmon which was in a basket under the seat, and that this was the secret of his pursuing us. This would be a terrific incident if it were a dead body that the crow scented, instead of a basket of salmon. Suppose, for instance, in a coach travelling along, that one of the passengers suddenly should die, and that one of the indications of his death would be this deportment of the crow.

July 29th.—Remarkable characters:—A disagreeable figure, waning from middle age, clad in a pair of tow homespun pantaloons, and a very soiled shirt, barefoot, and with one of his feet maimed by an axe; also an arm amputated two or three inches below the elbow. His beard of a week's growth, grim and grisly, with a general effect of black; altogether a disgusting object. Yet he has the signs of having been a handsome man in his idea, though now such a beastly figure that probably no living thing but his great dog would touch him without an effort. Coming to the stoop, where several persons were sitting, "Good morning, gentlemen," said the wretch. Nobody answered for a time, till at last one said, "I don't know whom you speak to: not to me, I'm sure" (meaning that he did not claim to be a gentleman). "Why, I thought I spoke to you all at once," replied the figure, laughing. So he sat himself down on the lower step of the stoop, and began to talk; and, the conversation being turned upon his bare feet by one of the company, he related the story of his losing his toes by the glancing aside of an axe, and with what great fortitude he bore it. Then he made a transition to the loss of his arm, and, setting his teeth and drawing in his breath, said that the pain was dreadful; but this, too, he seems to have borne like an Indian; and a person testified to his fortitude by saying that he did not suppose there was any feeling in him, from observing how he bore it. The man spoke of the pain of cutting the muscles, and the particular agony at one moment, while the bone was being sawed asunder; and there was a strange expression of remembered anguish, as he shrugged his half-limb, and described the matter. Afterwards, in a reply to a question of mine, whether he still seemed to feel the hand that had been amputated, he answered that he did always; and, baring the stump, he moved the severed muscles, saying, "There is the thumb, there the forefinger," and so on. Then he talked to me about phrenology, of which he seems a firm believer and skilful practitioner, telling how he had hit upon the true character of many people. There was a great deal of sense and acuteness in his talk, and something of elevation in his expressions,—perhaps a studied elevation,—and a sort of courtesy in his manner; but his sense had something out of the way in it; there was something wild and ruined and desperate in his talk, though I can hardly say what it was. There was a trace of the gentleman and man of intellect through his deep degradation; and a pleasure in intellectual pursuits, and an acuteness and trained judgment, which bespoke a mind once strong and cultivated. "My study is man," said he. And looking at me, "I do not know your name," he said, "but there is something of the hawk-eye about you, too."

This man was formerly a lawyer in good practice; but, taking to drinking, was reduced to the lowest state. Yet not the lowest; for after the amputation of his arm, being advised by divers persons to throw himself upon the public for support, he told them that, even if he should lose his other arm, he would still be able to support himself and a servant. Certainly he is a strong-minded and iron-constitutioned man; hut, looking at the stump of his arm, he said that the pain of the mind was a thousand times greater than the pain of the body. "That hand could make the pen go fast," said he. Among people in general, he does not seem to have any greater consideration in his ruin because of his former standing in society. He supports himself by making soap; and, on account of the offals used in that business, there is probably rather an evil odor in his domicile. Talking about a dead horse near his house, he said that he could not bear the scent of it. "I should not think you could smell carrion in that house," said a stage agent. Whereupon the soap-maker dropped his head, with a little snort, as it were, of wounded feeling; but immediately said that he took all in good part. There was an old squire of the village, a lawyer probably, whose demeanor was different,— with a distance, yet with a kindliness; for he remembered the times when they met on equal terms. "You and I," said the squire, alluding to their respective troubles and sicknesses, "would have died long ago, if we had not had the courage to live." The poor devil kept talking to me long after everybody else had left the stoop, giving vent to much practical philosophy, and just observation on the ways of men, mingled with rather more assumption of literature and cultivation than belonged to the present condition of his mind. Meantime his great dog, a cleanly looking and not ill-bred dog, being the only decent attribute appertaining to his master,—a well-natured dog, too, and receiving civilly any demonstration of courtesy from other people, though preserving a certain distance of deportment,—this great dog grew weary of his master's lengthy talk, and expressed his impatience to be gone by thrusting himself between his legs, rolling over on his back, seizing his ragged trousers, or playfully taking his maimed, bare foot into his mouth,—using, in short, the kindly and humorous freedom of a friend, with a wretch to whom all are free enough, but none other kind. His master rebuked him, but with kindness too, and not so that the dog felt himself bound to desist, though he seemed willing to allow his master all the time that could possibly be spared. And at last, having said many times that he must go and shave and dress himself,—and as his beard had been at least a week growing, it might have seemed almost a week's work to get rid of it,—he rose from the stoop and went his way,—a forlorn and miserable thing in the light of the cheerful summer morning. Yet he seems to keep his spirits up, and still preserves himself a man among men, asking nothing from them; nor is it clearly perceptible what right they have to scorn him, though he seems to acquiesce, in a manner, in their doing so. And yet he cannot wholly have lost his self-respect; and doubtless there were persons on the stoop more grovelling than himself.

Another character:—A blacksmith of fifty or upwards, a corpulent figure, big in the paunch and enormous in the rear; yet there is such an appearance of strength and robustness in his frame, that his corpulence appears very proper and necessary to him. A pound of flesh could not be spared from his abundance, any more than from the leanest man; and he walks about briskly, without any panting or symptom of labor or pain in his motion. He has a round, jolly face, always mirthful and humorous and shrewd, and the air of a man well to do, and well respected, yet not caring much about the opinions of men, because his independence is sufficient to itself. Nobody would take him for other than a man of some importance in the community, though his summer dress is a tow-cloth pair of pantaloons, a shirt not of the cleanest, open at the breast, and the sleeves rolled up at the elbows, and a straw hat. There is not such a vast difference between this costume and that of Lawyer H——— above mentioned, yet never was there a greater diversity of appearance than between these two men; and a glance at them would be sufficient to mark the difference. The blacksmith loves his glass, and comes to the tavern for it, whenever it seems good to him, not calling for it slyly and shyly, but marching steadily to the bar, or calling across the room for it to be prepared. He speaks with great bitterness against the new license law, and vows if it be not repealed by fair means it shall be by violence, and that he will be as ready to cock his rifle for such a cause as for any other. On this subject his talk is really fierce; but as to all other matters he is good-natured and good-hearted, fond of joke, and shaking his jolly sides with frequent laughter. His conversation has much strong, unlettered sense, imbued with humor, as everybody's talk is in New England.

He takes a queer position sometimes,—queer for his figure particularly, —straddling across a chair, facing the back, with his arms resting thereon, and his chin on them, for the benefit of conversing closely with some one. When he has spent as much time in the bar-room or under the stoop as he chooses to spare, he gets up at once, and goes off with a brisk, vigorous pace. He owns a mill, and seems to be prosperous in the world. I know no man who seems more like a man, more indescribably human, than this sturdy blacksmith.

There came in the afternoon a respectable man in gray homespun cloth, who arrived in a wagon, I believe, and began to inquire, after supper, about a certain new kind of mill machinery. Being referred to the blacksmith, who owned one of these mills, the stranger said that he had come from Vermont to learn about the matter. "What may I call your name?" said he to the blacksmith. "My name is Hodge," replied the latter. "I believe I have heard of you," said the stranger. Then they colloquied at much length about the various peculiarities and merits of the new invention. The stranger continued here two or three days, making his researches, and forming acquaintance with several millwrights and others. He was a man evidently of influence in his neighborhood, and the tone of his conversation was in the style of one accustomed to be heard with deference, though all in a plain and homely way. Lawyer H——— took notice of this manner; for the talk being about the nature of soap, and the evil odor arising from that process, the stranger joined in. "There need not be any disagreeable smell in making soap," said he. "Now we are to receive a lesson," said H———, and the remark was particularly apropos to the large wisdom of the stranger's tone and air.

Then he gave an account of the process in his domestic establishment, saying that he threw away the whole offals of the hog, as not producing any soap, and preserved the skins of the intestines for sausages. He seemed to be hospitable, inviting those with whom he did business to take "a mouthful of dinner" with him, and treating them with liquors; for he was not an utter temperance man, though moderate in his potations. I suspect he would turn out a pattern character of the upper class of New England yeomen, if I had an opportunity of studying him. Doubtless he had been selectman, representative, and justice, and had filled all but weighty offices. He was highly pleased with the new mill contrivance, and expressed his opinion that, when his neighbors saw the success of his, it would be extensively introduced into that vicinity.

Mem. The hostlers at taverns call the money given them "pergasus,"— corrupted from "perquisites." Otherwise "knock-down money." Remarkable character:—A travelling surgeon-dentist, who has taken a room in the North Adams House, and sticks up his advertising bills on the pillars of the piazza, and all about the town. He is a tall, slim young man, six feet two, dressed in a country-made coat of light blue (taken, as he tells me, in exchange for dental operations), black pantaloons, and clumsy, cowhide boots. Self-conceit is very strongly expressed in his air; and a doctor once told him that he owed his life to that quality; for, by keeping himself so stiffly upright, he opens his chest, and counteracts a consumptive tendency. He is not only a dentist, which trade he follows temporarily, but a licensed preacher of the Baptist persuasion, and is now on his way to the West to seek a place of settlement in his spiritual vocation. Whatever education he possesses, he has acquired by his own exertions since the age of twenty-one,—he being now twenty-four. We talk together very freely; and he has given me an account, among other matters, of all his love-affairs, which are rather curious, as illustrative of the life of a smart young country fellow in relation to the gentle sex. Nothing can exceed the exquisite self-conceit which characterizes these confidences, and which is expressed inimitably in his face, his upturned nose, and mouth, so as to be truly a caricature; and he seems strangely to find as much food for his passion in having been jilted once or twice as in his conquests. It is curious to notice his revengeful feeling against the false ones,— hidden from himself, however, under the guise of religious interest, and desire that they may be cured of their follies.

A little boy named Joe, who haunts about the bar-room and the stoop, four years old, in a thin, short jacket, and full-breeched trousers, and bare feet. The men tease him, and put quids of tobacco in his mouth, under pretence of giving him a fig; and he gets curaged, and utters a peculiar, sharp, spiteful cry, and strikes at them with a stick, to their great mirth. He is always in trouble, yet will not keep away. They despatch him with two or three cents to buy candy and nuts and raisins. They set him down in a niche of the door, and tell him to remain there a day and a half: he sits down very demurely, as if he meant to fulfil his penance; but a moment after, behold! there is little Joe capering across the street to join two or three boys who are playing in a wagon. Take this boy as the germ of a tavern-haunter, a country roue, to spend a wild and brutal youth, ten years of his prime in the State Prison, and his old age in the poorhouse.

There are a great many dogs kept in the village, and many of the travellers also have dogs. Some are almost always playing about; and if a cow or a pig be passing, two or three of them scamper forth for an attack. Some of the younger sort chase pigeons, wheeling as they wheel. If a contest arises between two dogs, a number of others come with huge barking to join the fray, though I believe that they do not really take any active part in the contest, but swell the uproar by way of encouraging the combatants. When a traveller is starting from the door, his dog often gets in front of the horse, placing his forefeet down,— looking the horse in the face, and barking loudly, then, as the horse comes on, running a little farther, and repeating the process; and this he does in spite of his master's remonstrances, till, the horse being fairly started, the dog follows on quietly. One dog, a diminutive little beast, has been taught to stand on his hind legs, and rub his face with his paw, which he does with an aspect of much endurance and deprecation. Another springs at people whom his master points out to him, barking and pretending to bite. These tricks make much mirth in the bar-room. All dogs, of whatever different sizes and dissimilar varieties, acknowledge the common bond of species among themselves, and the largest one does not disdain to suffer his tail to be smelt of, nor to reciprocate that courtesy to the smallest. They appear to take much interest in one another; but there is always a degree of caution between two strange dogs when they meet.

July 31st.—A visit to what is called "Hudson's Cave," or "Hudson's Falls," the tradition being that a man by the name of Henry Hudson, many years ago, chasing a deer, the deer fell over the place, which then first became known to white men. It is not properly a cave, but a fissure in a huge ledge of marble, through which a stream has been for ages forcing its way, and has left marks of its gradually wearing power on the tall crags, having made curious hollows from the summit down to the level which it has reached at the present day. The depth of the fissure in some places is at least fifty or sixty feet, perhaps more, and at several points it nearly closes over, and often the sight of the sky is hidden by the interposition of masses of the marble crags. The fissure is very irregular, so as not to be describable in words, and scarcely to be painted,—jetting buttresses, moss-grown, impending crags, with tall trees growing on their verge, nodding over the head of the observer at the bottom of the chasm, and rooted, as it were, in air. The part where the water works its way down is very narrow; but the chasm widens, after the descent, so as to form a spacious chamber between the crags, open to the sky, and its floor is strewn with fallen fragments of marble, and trees that have been precipitated long ago, and are heaped with drift-wood, left there by the freshets, when the scanty stream becomes a considerable waterfall. One crag, with a narrow ridge, which might be climbed without much difficulty, protrudes from the middle of the rock, and divides the fall. The passage through the cave made by the stream is very crooked, and interrupted, not only by fallen wrecks,

101

but by deep pools of water, which probably have been forded by few. As the deepest pool occurs in the most uneven part of the chasm, where the hollows in the sides of the crag are deepest, so that each hollow is almost a cave by itself, I determined to wade through it. There was an accumulation of soft stuff on the bottom, so that the water did not look more than knee-deep; but, finding that my feet sunk in it, I took off my trousers, and waded through up to my middle. Thus I reached the most interesting part of the cave, where the whirlings of the stream had left the marks of its eddies in the solid marble, all up and down the two sides of the chasm. The water is now dammed for the construction of two marble saw-mills, else it would have been impossible to effect the passage; and I presume that, for years after the cave was discovered, the waters roared and tore their way in a torrent through this part of the chasm. While I was there, I heard voices, and a small stone tumbled down; and looking up towards the narrow strip of bright light, and the sunny verdure that peeped over the top,—looking up thither from the deep, gloomy depth,—I saw two or three men; and, not liking to be to them the most curious part of the spectacle, I waded back, and put on my clothes. The marble crags are overspread with a concretion, which makes them look as gray as granite, except where the continual flow of water keeps them of a snowy whiteness. If they were so white all over, it would be a splendid show. There is a marble-quarry close in the rear, above the cave, and in process of time the whole of the crags will be quarried into tombstones, doorsteps, fronts of edifices, fireplaces, etc. That will be a pity. On such portions of the walls as are within reach, visitors have sculptured their initials, or names at full length; and the white letters showing plainly on the gray surface, they have more obvious effect than such inscriptions generally have. There was formerly, I believe, a complete arch of marble, forming a natural bridge over the top of the cave; but this is no longer so. At the bottom of the broad chamber of the cave, standing in its shadow, the effect of the morning sunshine on the dark or bright foliage of the pines and other trees that cluster on the summits of the crags was particularly beautiful; and it was strange how such great trees had rooted themselves in solid marble, for so it seemed.

After passing through this romantic and most picturesque spot, the stream goes onward to turn factories. Here its voice resounds within the hollow crags; there it goes onward; talking to itself, with babbling din, of its own wild thoughts and fantasies,—the voice of solitude and the wilderness,— loud and continual, but which yet does not seem to disturb the thoughtful wanderer, so that he forgets there is a noise. It talks along its storm-strewn path; it talks beneath tall precipices and high banks,—a voice that has been the same for innumerable ages; and yet, if you listen, you will perceive a continual change and variety in its babble, and sometimes it seems to swell louder upon the ear than at others,—in the same spot, I mean. By and by man makes a dam for it, and it pours over it, still making its voice heard, while it labors. At one shop for manufacturing the marble, I saw the disk of a sun-dial as large as the top of a hogshead, intended for Williams College; also a small obelisk, and numerous gravestones. The marble is coarse-grained, but of a very brilliant whiteness. It is rather a pity that the cave is not formed of some worthless stone.

In the deep valleys of the neighborhood, where the shadows at sunset are thrown from mountain to mountain, the clouds have a beautiful effect, flitting high over them, bright with heavenly gold. It seems as if the soul might rise up from the gloom, and alight upon them and soar away. Walking along one of the valleys the other evening, while a pretty fresh breeze blew across it, the clouds that were skimming over my head seemed to conform themselves to the valley's shape.

At a distance, mountain summits look close together, almost as if forming one mountain, though in reality a village lies in the depths between them.

A steam-engine in a factory to be supposed to possess a malignant spirit. It catches one man's arm, and pulls it off; seizes another by the coat-tails, and almost grapples him bodily; catches a girl by the hair, and scalps her; and finally draws in a man, and crushes him to death.

The one-armed soap-maker, Lawyer H———, wears an iron hook, which serves him instead of a hand for the purpose of holding on. They nickname him "Black Hawk."

North Adams still.—The village, viewed from the top of a hill to the westward at sunset, has a peculiarly happy and peaceful look. It lies on a level, surrounded by hills, and seems as if it lay in the hollow of a large hand. The Union Village may be seen, a manufacturing place, extending up a gorge of the hills. It is amusing to see all the distributed property of the aristocracy and commonalty, the various and conflicting interests of the town, the loves and hates, compressed into a space which the eye takes in as completely as the arrangement of a tea-table. The rush of the streams comes up the hill somewhat like the sound of a city.

The hills about the village appear very high and steep sometimes, when the shadows of the clouds are thrown blackly upon them, while there is sunshine elsewhere; so that, seen in front, the effect of their gradual slope is lost. These hills, surrounding the town on all sides, give it a snug and insulated air; and, viewed from certain points, it would be difficult to tell how to get out, without climbing the mountain ridges; but the roads wind away and accomplish the passage without ascending very high. Sometimes the notes of a horn or bugle may be heard sounding afar among these passes of the mountains, announcing the coming of the stage-coach from Bennington or Troy or Greenfield or Pittsfield.

There are multitudes of sheep among the hills, and they appear very tame and gentle; though sometimes, like the wicked, they "flee when no man pursueth." But, climbing a rude, rough, rocky, stumpy, ferny height yesterday, one or two of them stood and stared at me with great earnestness. I passed on quietly, but soon heard an immense baa-ing up the hill, and all the sheep came galloping and scrambling after me, baa-ing with all their might in innumerable voices, running in a compact body, expressing the utmost eagerness, as if they sought the greatest imaginable favor from me; and so they accompanied me down the hillside,— a most ridiculous cortege. Doubtless they had taken it into their heads that I brought them salt.

The aspect of the village is peculiarly beautiful towards sunset, when there are masses of cloud about the sky,—the remnants of a thunder-storm These clouds throw a shade upon large portions of the rampart of hills, and the hills towards the west are shaded of course; the clouds also make the shades deeper in the village, and thus the sunshine on the houses and trees, and along the street, is a bright, rich gold. The green is deeper in consequence of the recent rain.

The doctors walk about the village with their saddle-bags on their arms, one always with a pipe in his mouth.

A little dog, named Snapper, the same who stands on his hind legs, appears to be a roguish little dog, and the other day he stole one of the servant-girl's shoes, and ran into the street with it. Being pursued, he would lift the shoe in his mouth (while it almost dragged on the ground), and run a little way, then lie down with his paws on it, and wait to be pursued again.

August 11th.—This morning, it being cloudy and boding of rain, the clouds had settled upon the mountains, both on the summits and ridges, all round the town, so that there seemed to be no way of gaining access to the rest of the world, unless by climbing above the clouds. By and by they partially dispersed, giving glimpses of the mountain ramparts through their obscurity, the separate clouds lying heavily upon the mountain's breast. In warm mornings, after rain, the mist breaks forth from the forests on the ascent of the mountains, like smoke,—the smoke of a volcano; then it soars up, and becomes a cloud in heaven. But these clouds to-day were real rain-clouds. Sometimes, it is said, while laboring up the mountain-side, they suddenly burst, and pour down their moisture in a cataract, sweeping all before it.

Every new aspect of the mountains, or view from a different position, creates a surprise in the mind.

Scenes and characters:—A young country fellow, twenty or thereabouts, decently dressed, pained with the toothache. A doctor, passing on horseback, with his black leather saddle-bags behind him, a thin, frosty-haired man. Being asked to operate, he looks at the tooth, lances the gum, and the fellow being content to be dealt with on the spot, he seats himself in a chair on the stoop with great heroism. The doctor produces a rusty pair of iron forceps; a man holds the patient's head; the doctor perceives that, it being a difficult tooth to get at, wedged between the two largest in his jaws, he must pull very hard; and the instrument is introduced. A turn of the doctor's hand; the patient begins to utter a cry, but the tooth comes out first, with four prongs. The patient gets up, half amazed, pays the doctor ninepence, pockets the tooth, and the spectators are in glee and admiration.

There was a fat woman, a stage-passenger to-day,—a wonder how she could possibly get through the door, which seemed not so wide as she. When she put her foot on the step, the stage gave a great lurch, she joking all the while. A great, coarse, red-faced dame. Other passengers,—three or four slender Williamstown students, a young girl, and a man with one leg and two crutches.

One of the most sensible men in this village is a plain, tall, elderly person, who is overseeing the mending of a road,—humorous, intelligent, with much thought about matters and things; and while at work he has a sort of dignity in handling the hoe or crow-bar, which shows him to be the chief. In the evening he sits under the stoop, silent and observant from under the brim of his hat; but, occasion calling, he holds an argument about the benefit or otherwise of manufactories or other things. A simplicity characterizes him more than appertains to most Yankees.

A man in a pea-green frock-coat, with velvet collar. Another in a flowered chintz frock-coat. There is a great diversity of hues in garments. A doctor, a stout, tall, round-paunched, red-faced, brutal-looking old fellow, who gets drunk daily. He sat down on the step of our stoop, looking surly, and speaking to nobody; then got up and walked homeward, with a morose swagger and a slight unevenness of gait, attended by a fine Newfoundland dog.

A barouche with driver returned from beyond Greenfield or Troy empty, the passengers being left at the former place. The driver stops here for the night, and, while washing, enters into talk with an old man about the different roads over the mountain.

People washing themselves at a common basin in the bar-room! and using the common hair-brushes! perhaps with a consciousness of praiseworthy neatness!

A man with a cradle on his shoulder, having been cradling oats. I attended a child's funeral yesterday afternoon. There was an assemblage of people in a plain, homely apartment. Most of the men were dressed in their ordinary clothes, and one or two were in shirt-sleeves. The coffin was placed in the midst of us, covered with a velvet pall. A bepaid clergyman prayed (the audience remaining seated, while he stood up at the head of the coffin), read a passage of Scripture and commented upon it. While he read and prayed and expounded there was a heavy thunder-storm rumbling among the surrounding hills, and the lightning flashed fiercely through the gloomy room; and the preacher alluded to GOD's voice of thunder.

It is the custom in this part of the country—and perhaps extensively in the interior of New England—to bury the dead first in a charnel-house, or common tomb, where they remain till decay has so far progressed as to secure them from the resurrectionists. They are then reburied, with certain ceremonies, in their own peculiar graves.

O. E. S———, a widower of forty or upwards, with a son of twelve and a pair of infant twins. He is a sharp, shrewd Yankee, with a Yankee's license of honesty. He drinks sometimes more than enough, and is guilty of peccadilloes with the fair sex; yet speaks most affectionately of his wife, and is a fond and careful father. He is a tall, thin, hard-featured man, with a sly expression of almost hidden grave humor, as if there were some deviltry pretty constantly in his mind,—which is probably the case. His brother tells me that he was driven almost crazy by the loss of his wife. It appears to me that men are more affected by the deaths of their wives than wives by the deaths of their husbands. Orrin S——— smokes a pipe, as do many of the guests.

A walk this forenoon up the mountain ridge that walls in the town towards the east. The road is cut zigzag, the mountain being generally as steep as the roof of a house; yet the stage to Greenfield passes over this road two or three times a week. Graylock rose up behind me, appearing, with its two summits and a long ridge between, like a huge monster crouching down slumbering, with its head slightly elevated. Graylock is properly the name for the highest elevation. It appeared to better advantage the higher the point from which I viewed it. There were houses scattered here and there up the mountainside, growing poorer as I ascended; the last that I passed was a mean log-hut, rough, rude, and dilapidated, with the smoke issuing from a chimney of small stones, plastered with clay; around it a garden of beans, with some attempt at flowers, and a green creeper running over the side of the cottage. Above this point there were various excellent views of mountain scenery, far off and near, and one village lying below in the hollow vale.

Having climbed so far that the road seemed now to go downward, I retraced my steps. There was a wagon descending behind me; and as it followed the zigzag of the road I could hear the voices of the men high over my head, and sometimes I caught a glimpse of the wagon almost perpendicularly above me, while I was looking almost perpendicularly down to the log-hut aforementioned. Trees were thick on either hand,—oaks, pines, and others; and marble occasionally peeped up in the road and there was a lime-kiln by the wayside, ready for burning.

Graylock had a cloud on his head this morning, the base of a heavy white cloud. The distribution of the sunshine amid mountain scenery is very striking; one does not see exactly why one spot should be in deep obscurity while others are all bright. The clouds throw their shadows upon the hillsides as they move slowly along,—a transitory blackness.

I passed a doctor high up the road in a sulky, with his black leather saddle-bags.

Hudson's Cave is formed by Hudson's Brook. There is a natural arch of marble still in one part of it. The cliffs are partly made verdant with green moss, chiefly gray with oxidation; on some parts the white of the marble is seen; in interstices grow brake and other shrubs, so that there is naked sublimity seen through a good deal of clustering beauty. Above, the birch, poplars, and pines grow on the utmost verge of the cliffs, which jut far over, so that they are suspended in air; and whenever the sunshine finds its way into the depths of the chasm, the branches wave across it. There is a lightness, however, about their foliage, which greatly relieves what would otherwise be a gloomy scene. After the passage of the stream through the cliffs of marble, the cliffs separate on either side, and leave it to flow onward; intercepting its passage, however, by fragments of marble, some of them huge ones, which the cliffs have flung down, thundering into the bed of the stream through numberless ages. Doubtless some of these immense fragments had trees growing on them, which have now mouldered away. Decaying trunks are heaped in various parts of the gorge. The pieces of marble that are washed by the water are of a snow-white, and partially covered with a bright green water-moss, making a beautiful contrast.

Among the cliffs, strips of earth-beach extend downward, and trees and large shrubs root themselves in that earth, thus further contrasting the nakedness of the stone with their green foliage. But the immediate part where the stream forces its winding passage through the rock is stern, dark, and mysterious.

Along the road, where it runs beneath a steep, there are high ridges, covered with trees,—the dew of midnight damping the earth, far towards midnoon. I observed the shadows of water-insects, as they swam in the pools of a stream. Looking down a streamlet, I saw a trunk of a tree, which has been overthrown by the wind, so as to form a bridge, yet sticking up all its branches, as if it were unwilling to assist anybody over.

Green leaves, following the eddies of the rivulet, were now borne deep under water, and now emerged. Great uprooted trees, adhering midway down a precipice of earth, hung with their tops downward.

There is an old man, selling the meats of butternuts under the stoop of the hotel. He makes that his station during a part of the season. He was dressed in a dark thin coat, ribbed velvet pantaloons, and a sort of moccasins, or shoes, appended to the legs of woollen stockings. He had on a straw hat, and his hair was gray, with a long, thin visage. His nuts were contained in a square tin box, having two compartments, one for the nuts, and another for maple sugar, which he sells in small cakes. He had three small tin measures for nuts,—one at one cent, others at two, four, and six cents; and as fast as they were emptied, he filled them again, and put them on the top of his box. He smoked a pipe, and talked with one man about whether it would be worth while to grow young again, and the duty of being contented with old age;

about predestination and freewill and other metaphysics. I asked him what his sales amounted to in the course of a day. He said that butternuts did not sell so well as walnuts, which are not yet in season; that he might to-day have sold fifty cents' worth of walnuts, never less than a dollar's worth, often more; and when he went round with a caravan, he had sold fifteen dollars' worth per day, and once as much as twenty dollars' worth. This promises to be an excellent year for walnuts. Chestnuts have been scarce for two or three years. He had one hundred chestnut-trees on his own land, and last year he offered a man twenty-five cents if he would find him a quart of good chestnuts on them. A bushel of walnuts would cost about ten dollars. He wears a pair of silver-rimmed spectacles.

A drunken fellow sat down by him, and bought a cent's worth of his butternuts, and inquired what he would sell out to him for. The old man made an estimate, though evidently in jest, and then reckoned his box, measures, meats, and what little maple sugar he had, at four dollars. He had a very quiet manner, and expressed an intention of going to the Commencement at Williamstown to-morrow. His name, I believe, is Captain Gavett.

Wednesday, August 15th.—I went to Commencement at Williams College,— five miles distant. At the tavern were students with ribbons, pink or blue, fluttering from their buttonholes, these being the badges of rival societies. There was a considerable gathering of people, chiefly arriving in wagons or buggies, some in barouches, and very few in chaises. The most characteristic part of the scene was where the pedlers, gingerbread-sellers, etc., were collected, a few hundred yards from the meeting-house. There was a pedler there from New York State, who sold his wares by auction, and I could have stood and listened to him all day long. Sometimes he would put up a heterogeny [this is a word made by Mr. Hawthorne, but one that was needed.—S. H.] of articles in a lot,—as a paper of pins, a lead-pencil, and a shaving-box,—and knock them all down, perhaps for ninepence. Bunches of lead-pencils, steel-pens, pound-cakes of shaving-soap, gilt finger-rings bracelets, clasps, and other jewelry, cards of pearl buttons, or steel ("there is some steel about them, gentlemen, for my brother stole 'em, and I bore him out in it"), bundles of wooden combs, boxes of matches, suspenders

110

and, in short, everything,—dipping his hand down into his wares with the promise of a wonderful lot, and producing, perhaps, a bottle of opodeldoc, and joining it with a lead-pencil,—and when he had sold several things of the same kind, pretending huge surprise at finding "just one more," if the lads lingered; saying, "I could not afford to steal them for the price; for the remorse of conscience would be worth more,"—all the time keeping an eye upon those who bought, calling for the pay, making change with silver or bills, and deciding on the goodness of banks; and saying to the boys who climbed upon his cart, "Fall down, roll down, tumble down, only get down"; and uttering everything in the queer, humorous recitative in which he sold his articles. Sometimes he would pretend that a person had bid, either by word or wink, and raised a laugh thus; never losing his self-possession, nor getting out of humor. When a man asked whether a bill were good: "No! do you suppose I'd give you good money?" When he delivered an article, he exclaimed, "You're the lucky man," setting off his wares with the most extravagant eulogies. The people bought very freely, and seemed also to enjoy the fun. One little boy bought a shaving-box, perhaps meaning to speculate upon it. This character could not possibly he overdrawn; and he was really excellent, with his allusions to what was passing, intermingled, doubtless, with a good deal that was studied. He was a man between thirty and forty, with a face expressive of other ability, as well as of humor.

A good many people were the better or the worse for liquor. There was one fellow,—named Randall, I think,—a round-shouldered, bulky, ill-hung devil, with a pale, sallow skin, black beard, and a sort of grin upon his face,—a species of laugh, yet not so much mirthful as indicating a strange mental and moral twist. He was very riotous in the crowd, elbowing, thrusting, seizing hold of people; and at last a ring was formed, and a regular wrestling-match commenced between him and a farmer-looking man. Randall brandished his legs about in the most ridiculous style, but proved himself a good wrestler, and finally threw his antagonist. He got up with the same grin upon his features,—not a grin of simplicity, but intimating knowingness. When more depth or force of expression was required, he could put on the most strangely ludicrous and ugly aspect (suiting his gesture and attitude to it) that can be imagined. I should like to see this fellow when he was perfectly sober.

There were a good many blacks among the crowd. I suppose they used to emigrate across the border, while New York was a slave State. There were enough of them to form a party, though greatly in the minority; and, a squabble arising, some of the blacks were knocked down, and otherwise maltreated. I saw one old negro, a genuine specimen of the slave negro, without any of the foppery of the race in our part of the State,—an old fellow, with a bag, I suppose of broken victuals, on his shoulder, and his pockets stuffed out at his hips with the like provender; full of grimaces and ridiculous antics, laughing laughably, yet without affectation; then talking with a strange kind of pathos about the whippings he used to get while he was a slave;—a singular creature, of mere feeling, with some glimmering of sense. Then there was another gray old negro, but of a different stamp, politic, sage, cautious, yet with boldness enough, talking about the rights of his race, yet so as not to provoke his audience; discoursing of the advantage of living under laws, and the wonders that might ensue, in that very assemblage, if there were no laws; in the midst of this deep wisdom, turning off the anger of a half-drunken fellow by a merry retort, a leap in the air, and a negro's laugh. I was interested—there being a drunken negro ascending the meeting-house steps, and near him three or four well-dressed and decent negro wenches—to see the look of scorn and shame and sorrow and painful sympathy which one of them assumed at this disgrace of her color.

The people here show out their character much more strongly than they do with us; there was not the quiet, silent, dull decency of our public assemblages, but mirth, anger, eccentricity,—all manifesting themselves freely. There were many watermelons for sale, and people burying their muzzles deep in the juicy flesh of them. There were cider and beer. Many of the people had their mouths half opened in a grin, which, more than anything else, I think, indicates a low stage of refinement. A low-crowned hat—very low—is common. They are respectful to gentlemen.

A bat being startled, probably, out of the meeting-house, by the commotion around, flew blindly about in the sunshine, and alighted on a man's sleeve. I looked at him,—a droll, winged, beast-insect, creeping up the man's arm, not over-clean, and scattering dust on the man's coat from his vampire wings. The man stared at him, and let the spectators stare for a minute, and then shook him gently off; and the poor devil took a flight across the green to the meeting-house, and then, I believe, alighted on somebody else. Probably he was put to death. Bats are very numerous in these parts.

There was a drunken man, annoying people with his senseless talk and impertinences, impelled to perform eccentricities by an evil spirit in him; and a pale little boy, with a bandaged leg, whom his father brought out of the tavern and put into a barouche. Then the boy heedfully placed shawls and cushions about his leg to support it, his face expressive of pain and care,—not transitory, but settled pain, of long and forcedly patient, endurance; and this painful look, perhaps, gave his face more intelligence than it might otherwise have had, though it was naturally a sensitive face. Well-dressed ladies were in the meeting-house in silks and cambrics,—the sunburnt necks in contiguity with the delicate fabrics of the dresses showing the yeomen's daughters.

Country graduates,—rough, brown-featured, schoolmaster-looking, half-bumpkin, half-scholarly figures, in black ill-cut broadcloth,—their manners quite spoilt by what little of the gentleman there was in them.

The landlord of the tavern keeping his eye on a man whom he suspected of an intention to bolt. [A word meaning in Worcester, I find, "to spring out with speed and suddenness."—S. H.]

The next day after Commencement was bleak and rainy from midnight till midnight, and a good many guests were added to our table in consequence. Among them were some of the Williamstown students, gentlemanly young fellows, with a brotherly feeling for each other, a freedom about money concerns, a half-boyish, half-manly character; and my heart warmed to them. They took their departure—two for South Adams and two across the Green Mountains—in the midst of the rain. There was one of the graduates with his betrothed, and his brother-in-law and wife, who stayed during the day,—the graduate the very model of a country schoolmaster in his Sunday clothes, being his Commencement suit of black broadcloth and pumps. He is engaged as assistant teacher of the academy at Shelburne Falls. There was also the high sheriff of Berkshire, Mr. Twining, with a bundle of writs under his arm, and

113

some of them peeping out of his pockets. Also several Trojan men and women, who had been to Commencement. Likewise a young clergyman, graduate of Brown College, and student of the Divinity School at Cambridge. He had come across the Hoosic, or Green Mountains, about eighteen miles, on foot, from Charlemont, where he is preaching, and had been to Commencement. Knowing little of men and matters, and desiring to know more, he was very free in making acquaintance with people, but could not do it handsomely. A singular smile broke out upon his face on slight provocation. He was awkward in his manners, yet it was not an ungentlemanly awkwardness,— intelligent as respects book-learning, but much deficient in worldly tact. It was pleasant to observe his consciousness of this deficiency, and how he strove to remedy it by mixing as much as possible with people, and sitting almost all day in the bar-room to study character. Sometimes he would endeavor to contribute his share to the general amusement,—as by growling comically, to provoke and mystify a dog; and by some bashful and half-apropos observations.

In the afternoon there came a fresh bevy of students onward from Williamstown; but they made only a transient visit, though it was still raining. These were a rough-hewn, heavy set of fellows, from the hills and woods in this neighborhood,—great unpolished bumpkins, who had grown up farmer-boys, and had little of the literary man, save green spectacles and black broadcloth (which all of them had not), talking with a broad accent, and laughing clown-like, while sheepishness overspread all, together with a vanity at being students. One of the party was six feet seven inches high, and all his herculean dimensions were in proportion; his features, too, were cast in a mould suitable to his stature. This giant was not ill-looking, but of a rattier intelligent aspect. His motions were devoid of grace, but yet had a rough freedom, appropriate enough to such a figure. These fellows stayed awhile, talked uncouthly about college matters, and started in the great open wagon which had brought them and their luggage hither. We had a fire in the bar-room almost all day,—a great, blazing fire,—and it was pleasant to have this day of bleak November weather, and cheerful fireside talk, and wet garments smoking in the fireside heat, still in the summer-time. Thus the day wore on with a sort of heavy, lazy pleasantness; and night set in, still stormy.

114

In the morning it was cloudy, but did not rain, and I went with the little clergyman to Hudson's Cave. The stream which they call the North Branch, and into which Hudson's Brook empties, was much swollen, and tumbled and dashed and whitened over the rocks, and formed real cascades over the dams, and rushed fast along the side of the cliffs, which had their feet in it. Its color was deep brown, owing to the washing of the banks which the rain had poured into it. Looking back, we could see a cloud on Graylock; but on other parts of Saddle Mountain there were spots of sunshine, some of most glorious brightness, contrasting with the general gloom of the sky, and the deep shadow which lay on the earth.

We looked at the spot where the stream makes its entrance into the marble cliff, and it was (this morning, at least) the most striking view of the cave. The water dashed down in a misty cascade, through what looked like the portal of some infernal subterranean structure; and far within the portal we could see the mist and the falling water; and it looked as if, but for these obstructions of view, we might have had a deeper insight into a gloomy region.

After our return, the little minister set off for his eighteen miles' journey across the mountain; and I was occupied the rest of the forenoon with an affair of stealing—a woman of forty or upwards being accused of stealing a needle-case and other trifles from a factory-girl at a boarding-house. She came here to take passage in a stage; but Putnam, a justice of the peace, examined her and afterwards ordered her to be searched by Laura and Eliza, the chambermaid and table-waiter. Hereupon was much fun and some sympathy. They searched, and found nothing that they sought, though she gave up a pair of pantalets, which she pretended to have taken by mistake. Afterwards, she being in the parlor, I went in; and she immediately began to talk to me, giving me an account of the affair, speaking with the bitterness of a wronged person, with a sparkling eye, yet with great fluency and self-possession. She is a yellow, thin, and battered old thing, yet rather country-lady-like in aspect and manners. I heard Eliza telling another girl about it, under my window; and she seemed to think that the poor woman's reluctance to be searched arose from the poorness of her wardrobe and of the contents of her bandbox.

At parting, Eliza said to the girl, "What do you think I heard somebody say about you? That it was enough to make anybody's eyes start square out of their head to look at such red cheeks as yours." Whereupon the girl turned off the compliment with a laugh, and took her leave.

There is an old blind dog, recognizing his friends by the sense of smell. I observe the eager awkwardness with which he accomplishes the recognition, his carefulness in descending steps, and generally in his locomotion. He evidently has not forgotten that he once had the faculty of sight; for he turns his eyes with earnestness towards those who attract his attention, though the orbs are plainly sightless.

Here is an Englishman,—a thorough-going Tory and Monarchist,— upholding everything English, government, people, habits, education, manufactures, modes of living, and expressing his dislike of all Americanisms,— and this in a quiet, calm, reasonable way, as if it were quite proper to live in a country and draw his subsistence from it, and openly abuse it. He imports his clothes from England, and expatiates on the superiority of English boots, hats, cravats, etc. He is a man of unmalleable habits, and wears his dress of the same fashion as that of twenty years ago.

August 18th.—There has come one of the proprietors, or superintendents, of a caravan of animals,—a large, portly paunched, dark-complexioned, brandy-burnt, heavy-faced man of about fifty; with a diminutive nose in proportion to the size of his face,—thick lips; nevertheless he has the air of a man who has seen much, and derived such experience as was for his purpose. Also it is the air of a man not in a subordinate station, though vulgar and coarse. He arrived in a wagon, with a span of handsome gray horses, and ordered dinner. He had left his caravan at Worcester, and came from thence and over the mountain hither, to settle stopping-places for the caravan. The nearest place to this, I believe, was Charlemont; the penultimate at Greenfield. In stopping at such a village as this, they do not expect much profit, if any; but would be content with enough to pay their travelling expenses, while they look to gather gain at larger places. In this village, it seems, the selectmen had resolved not to license any public exhibition of the kind; and it was interesting to attend to the consultations whether it were feasible to overcome the objections, and what might be the best means. Orrin S—— and the chance passers-by took part in the discussion. The scruple is that the factory-girls, having ready money by them, spend it for these nonsenses, quitting their work; whereas, were it a mere farming-town, the caravan would take little in proportion to their spendings. The opinion generally was that the license could not be obtained; and the portly man's face grew darker and downcast at the prospect; and he took out a travelling-map, and looked it carefully over, to discover some other station. This is something like the planning of the march of an army. It was finally resolved to enlist the influence of a brother-in-law of the head selectman, and try to gain his consent. Whereupon the caravan-man and the brother-in-law (who, being a tavern-keeper, was to divide the custom of the caravan people with this house) went to make the attempt,—the caravan-man stalking along with stiff, awkward bulk and stature, yet preserving a respectability withal, though with somewhat of the blackguard. Before he went, he offered a wager of "a drink of rum to a thaw of tobacco" that he did not succeed. When he came back, there was a flush in his face and a sparkle in his eye that did not look like failure; but I know not what was the result. He took a glass of wine with the brother-in-law,—a grave, thin, frosty-haired, shrewd-looking yeoman, in his shirt-sleeves,—then ordered his horses, paid his bill, and drove off, accompanied still by the same yeoman, perhaps to get the permission of the other two selectmen. If he does not get a license here, he will try at Cheshire.

A fellow appears with a pink guard-chain and two breast-pins in his shirt,—one a masonic one of gold, with compass and square, and the other of colored glass, set in filigree brass,—and the shirt a soiled one.

A tendency to obesity is more common in this part of the country than I have noticed it elsewhere.

August 19th.—I drove with Orrin S—— last evening to an old farmer's house to get some chickens. Entering the kitchen, I observed a fireplace with rough stone jambs and back, and a marble hearth, cracked, and otherwise contrasting a roughness of workmanship with the value of the material. There was a clock without a case, the weights being visible, and the pendulum swinging in air,—and a coffee-mill fixed against the wall. A religious newspaper lay on the mantel-piece. The old farmer was reluctant to go after the fowls, declaring that it would be impossible to find them in the dark; but Orrin insisting, he lighted a lamp, and we all went together, and quickly found them, roosted about the wood-pile; whereupon Orrin speedily laid hands on five, and wrung their necks in a twinkling, they fluttering long after they should have been dead. When we had taken our departure, Orrin remarked, "How faint-hearted these old fellows are!" and it was a good observation; for it was the farmer's timorous age that made him doubt the practicability of catching the chickens, and it contrasted well with the persevering energy of the middle-aged Orrin. But Orrin inquired, somewhat dolefully, whether I should suppose that he himself bewailed the advances of age. It is a grievous point with him.

In the evening there was a strange fellow in the bar-room,—a sort of mock Methodist,—a cattle-drover, who had stopped here for the night with two cows and a Durham bull. All his talk turned upon religion, and he would ever and anon burst out in some strain of scriptural-styled eloquence, chanted through his nose, like an exhortation at a camp-meeting. A group of Universalists and no-religionists sat around him, making him their butt, and holding wild argument with him; and he strangely mingled humor with his enthusiasm, and enthusiasm with his humor, so that it was almost impossible to tell whether he were in jest or earnest. Probably it was neither, but an eccentricity, an almost monomania, that has grown upon him,—perhaps the result of strong religious excitement. And, having been a backslider, he is cursed with a half-frenzied humor. In the morning he talked in the same strain at breakfast, while quaffing fourteen cups of tea,—Eliza, all the while, as she supplied him, entreating him not to drink any more. After breakfast (it being the Sabbath) he drove his two cows and bull past the stoop, raising his stair, and running after them with strange, uncouth gestures; and the last word I heard from him was an exhortation: "Gentlemen, now all of you take your Bibles, and meditate on divine things,"—this being uttered with raised hands, and a Methodistical tone, intermingled, as was his expression, with something humorous; so that, to the last, the puzzle was still kept up, whether he was an enthusiast or a jester. He wore a suit of coarse brown cloth, cut in rather a Quaker fashion; and he had a large nose, and his face expressed enthusiasm and honor,—a sort of smile and twinkle of the eye, with wildness. He is excellent at a bargain; and if, in the midst of his ghostly exhortation, the talk were turned on cattle, he eagerly seized the topic and expatiated on it.

While this fellow was enumerating the Universalists in neighboring towns who had turned from their errors on their death-beds, some one exclaimed, "John Hodges! why, he isn't dead,—he's alive and well." Whereat there was a roar of laughter. While holding an argument at table, I heard him mutter to himself at something that his adversary said; and though I could not distinguish what it was, the tone did more to convince me of some degree of earnestness than aught beside. This character might be wrought into a strange portrait of something sad, terrific, and laughable.

The Sabbath wore away lazily, and therefore wickedly. The heavy caravan-man inquired for some book of light reading, and, having obtained an old volume of a literary paper, betook himself to the seat of his wagon, to read. At other times he smoked, and talked sensibly enough with anybody that offered. He is a man of sense, though not quick, and seems to be a fair man.

When he walks, he puts the thumb of each hand into the armhole of his waistcoat, and moves along stiffly, with a knock-kneed gait. His talk was chiefly of hotels, and such matters as a man, always travelling, without any purpose of observation for mental improvement, would be interested in. He spoke of his life as a hard one.

There was a Methodist quarterly meeting here, and a love-feast.

There is a fellow hereabout who refuses to pay six dollars for the coffin in which his wife was buried. She died about six months since, and I believe he is already engaged to another. He is young and rather comely, but has not a straightforward look.

One man plods along, looking always on the ground, without ever lifting his eyes to the mountain scenery, and forest, and clouds, above and around him. Another walks the street with a quick, prying eye, and sharp face,—the most, expressive possible of one on the lookout for gain,—of the most disagreeable class of Yankees. There is also a sour-looking, unwholesome

119

boy, the son of this man, whose voice is querulous and ill-natured, precisely suited to his aspect. So is his character.

We have another with Indian blood in him, and the straight, black hair,— something of the tawny skin and the quick, shining eye of the Indian. He seems reserved, but is not ill-natured when spoken to. There is so much of the white in him, that he gives the impression of belonging to a civilized race, which causes the more strange sensation on discovering that he has a wild lineage.

August 22d.—I walked out into what is called the Notch this forenoon, between Saddle Mountain and another. There are good farms in this Notch, although the ground is considerably elevated,—this morning, indeed, above the clouds; for I penetrated through one in reaching the higher region, although I found sunshine there. Graylock was hidden in clouds, and the rest of Saddle Mountain had one partially wreathed about it; but it was withdrawn before long. It was very beautiful cloud-scenery. The clouds lay on the breast of the mountain, dense, white, well-defined, and some of them were in such close vicinity that it seemed as if I could infold myself in them; while others, belonging to the same fleet, were floating through the blue sky above. I had a view of Williamstown at the distance of a few miles,—two or three, perhaps,—a white village and steeple in a gradual hollow, with high mountainous swells heaving themselves up, like immense, subsiding waves, far and wide around it. On these high mountain-waves rested the white summer clouds, or they rested as still in the air above; and they were formed in such fantastic shapes that they gave the strongest possible impression of being confounded or intermixed with the sky. It was like a day-dream to look at it; and the students ought to be day-dreamers, all of them,—when cloud-land is one and the same thing with the substantial earth. By degrees all these clouds flitted away, and the sultry summer sun burned on hill and valley. As I was walking home, an old man came down the mountain-path behind me in a wagon, and gave me a drive to the village. Visitors being few in the Notch, the women and girls looked from the windows after me; the men nodded and greeted me with a look of curiosity; and two little girls whom I met, bearing tin pails, whispered one another and smiled.

North Adams, August 23d.—The county commissioners held a court; in the bar-room yesterday afternoon, for the purpose of letting out the making of the new road over the mountain. The commissioners sat together in attitudes of some dignity, with one leg laid across another; and the people, to the number of twenty or thirty, sat round about with their hats on, in their shirt-sleeves, with but little, yet with some formality. Several had come from a distance to bid for the job. They sat with whips in their hands. The first bid was three dollars,—then there was a long silence,—then a bid of two dollars eighty-five cents, and finally it was knocked down at two eighteen, per rod. A disposition to bid was evidenced in one man by his joking on the bid of another.

After supper, as the sun was setting, a man passed by the door with a hand-organ, connected with which was a row of figures, such as dancers, pirouetting and turning, a lady playing on a piano, soldiers, a negro wench dancing, and opening and shutting a huge red mouth,—all these keeping time to the lively or slow tunes of the organ. The man had a pleasant, but sly, dark face; he carried his whole establishment on his shoulder, it being fastened to a staff which he rested on the ground when he performed. A little crowd of people gathered about him on the stoop, peeping over each other's heads with huge admiration,—fat Otis Hodge, and the tall stage-driver, and the little boys, all declaring that it was the masterpiece of sights. Some few coppers did the man obtain, as well as much praise. He had come over the high, solitary mountain, where for miles there could hardly be a soul to hear his music.

In the evening, a portly old commissioner, a cheerful man enough, was sitting reading the newspaper in the parlor, holding the candle between the newspaper and his eyes,—its rays glittering on his silver-bowed spectacles and silvery hair. A pensive mood of age had come upon him, and sometimes he heaved a long sigh, while he turned and re-turned the paper, and folded it for convenient reading. By and by a gentleman came to see him, and he talked with him cheerfully.

The fat old squire, whom I have mentioned more than once, is an odd figure, with his bluff, red face,—coarsely red,—set in silver hair,— his clumsy legs, which he moves in a strange straddle, using, I believe, a broomstick for a staff. The breadth of back of these fat men is truly a wonder.

A decent man, at table the other day, took the only remaining potato out of the dish, on the end of his knife, and offered his friend half of it!

The mountains look much larger and more majestic sometimes than at others,—partly because the mind may be variously disposed, so as to comprehend them more or less, and partly that an imperceptible (or almost so) haze adds a great deal to the effect. Saddleback often looks a huge, black mass,—black-green, or black-blue.

The cave makes a fresh impression upon me every time I visit it,—so deep, so irregular, so gloomy, so stern,—part of its walls the pure white of the marble,—others covered with a gray decomposition and with spots of moss, and with brake growing where there is a handful of earth. I stand and look into its depths at various points, and hear the roar of the stream re-echoing up. It is like a heart that has been rent asunder by a torrent of passion, which has raged and foamed, and left its ineffaceable traces; though now there is but a little rill of feeling at the bottom.

In parts, trees have fallen across the fissure,—trees with large trunks.

I bathed in the stream in this old, secluded spot, which I frequent for that purpose. To reach it, I cross one branch of the stream on stones, and then pass to the other side of a little island, overgrown with trees and underbrush. Where I bathe, the stream has partially dammed itself up by sweeping together tree-trunks and slabs and branches, and a thousand things that have come down its current for years perhaps; so that there is a deep pool, full of eddies and little whirlpools which would carry me away, did I not take hold of the stem of a small tree that lies opportunely transversely across the water. The bottom is uneven, with rocks of various size, against which it is difficult to keep from stumbling, so rapid is the stream. Sometimes it bears along branches and strips of bark,—sometimes a green leaf, or perchance a dry one,— occasionally overwhelmed by the eddies and borne deep under water, then rushing atop the waves.

The forest, bordering the stream, produces its effect by a complexity of causes,—the old and stern trees, with stately trunks and dark foliage,— as the almost black pines,—the young trees, with lightsome green foliage,—as sapling oaks, maples and poplars,—then the old, decayed trunks, that are seen lying here and there, all mouldered, so that the foot would sink into them. The sunshine, falling capriciously on a casual branch considerably within the forest verge, while it leaves nearer trees in shadow, leads the imagination into the depths. But it soon becomes bewildered there. Rocks strewn about, half hidden in the fallen leaves, must not be overlooked.

August 26th.—A funeral last evening, nearly at sunset,—a coffin of a boy about ten years old laid on a one-horse wagon among some straw,—two or three barouches and wagons following. As the funeral passed through the village street, a few men formed a short procession in front of the coffin, among whom were Orrin S——- and I. The burial-ground (there are two in the town) is on the sides and summit of a round hill, which is planted with cypress and other trees, among which the white marble gravestones show pleasantly. The grave was dug on the steep slope of a hill; and the grave-digger was waiting there, and two or three other shirt-sleeved yeomen, leaning against the trees.

Orrin S———, a wanton and mirth-making middle-aged man, who would not seem to have much domestic feeling, took a chief part on the occasion, assisting in taking the coffin from the wagon and in lowering it into the grave. There being some superfluous earth at the bottom of the grave, the coffin was drawn up again after being once buried, and the obstacle removed with a hoe; then it was lowered again for the last time. While this was going on, the father and mother stood weeping at the upper end of the grave, at the head of the little procession,—the mother sobbing with stifled violence, and peeping forth to discover why the coffin was drawn up again. It being fitted in its place, Orrin S——— strewed some straw upon it,—this being the custom here, because "the clods on the coffin-lid have an ugly sound." Then the Baptist minister, having first whispered to the father, removed his hat, the spectators all doing the same, and thanked them "in the name of these mourners, for this last act of kindness to them."

In all these rites Orrin S——— bore the chief part with real feeling and sadly decorous demeanor. After the funeral, I took a walk on the Williamstown road, towards the west. There had been a heavy shower in the afternoon, and clouds were brilliant all over the sky, around Graylock and everywhere else. Those over the hills of the west were the most splendid in purple and gold, and, there being a haze, it added immensely to their majesty and dusky magnificence.

This morning I walked a little way along the mountain road, and stood awhile in the shadow of some oak and chestnut trees,—it being a warm, bright, sunshiny morning. The shades lay long from trees and other objects, as at sunset, but how different this cheerful and light radiance from the mild repose of sunset! Locusts, crickets, and other insects were making music. Cattle were feeding briskly, with morning appetites. The wakeful voices of children were heard in a neighboring hollow. The dew damped the road, and formed many-colored drops in the grass. In short, the world was not weary with a long, sultry day, but in a fresh, recruited state, fit to carry it through such a day.

A rough-looking, sunburnt, soiled-skirted, odd, middle-aged little man came to the house a day or two ago, seeking work. He had come from Ohio, and was returning to his native place, somewhere in New England, stopping occasionally to earn money to pay his way. There was something rather ludicrous in his physiognomy and aspect. He was very free to talk with all and sundry. He made a long eulogy on his dog Tiger, yesterday, insisting on his good moral character, his not being quarrelsome, his docility, and all other excellent qualities that a huge, strong, fierce mastiff could have. Tiger is the bully of the village, and keeps all the other dogs in awe. His aspect is very spirited, trotting massively along, with his tail elevated and his head likewise. "When he sees a dog that's anything near his size, he's apt to growl a little,"— Tiger had the marks of a battle on him,—"yet he's a good dog."

Friday, August 31st.—A drive on Tuesday to Shelburne Falls, twenty-two miles or thereabouts distant. Started at about eight o'clock in a wagon with Mr. Leach and Mr. Birch. Our road lay over the Green Mountains, the long ridge of which was made awful by a dark, heavy, threatening cloud, apparently rolled and condensed along the whole summit. As we ascended the zigzag road, we looked behind, at every opening in the forest, and beheld a wide landscape of mountain-swells and valleys intermixed, and old Graylock and the whole of Saddleback. Over the wide scene there was a general gloom; but there was a continual vicissitude of bright sunshine flitting over it, now resting for a brief space on portions of the heights, now flooding the valleys with green brightness, now making out distinctly each dwelling, and the hotels, and then two small brick churches of the distant village, denoting its prosperity, while all around seemed under adverse fortunes. But we, who stood so elevated above mortal things, and saw so wide and far, could see the sunshine of prosperity departing from one spot and rolling towards another, so that we could not think it much matter which spot were sunny or gloomy at any one moment.

The top of this Hoosic Mountain is a long ridge, marked on the county map as two thousand one hundred and sixty feet above the sea; on this summit is a valley, not very deep, but one or two miles wide, in which is the town of L———. Here there are respectable farmers, though it is a rough, and must be a bleak place. The first house, after reaching the summit, is a small, homely tavern. We left our horse in the shed, and, entering the little unpainted bar-room, we heard a voice, in a strange, outlandish accent, exclaiming "Diorama." It was an old man, with a full, gray-bearded countenance, and Mr. Leach exclaimed, "Ah, here's the old Dutchman again!" And he answered, "Yes, Captain, here's the old Dutchman,"—though, by the way, he is a German, and travels the country with this diorama in a wagon, and had recently been at South Adams, and was now returning from Saratoga Springs. We looked through the glass orifice of his machine, while he exhibited a succession of the very worst scratches and daubings that can be imagined,—worn out, too, and full of cracks and wrinkles, dimmed with tobacco-smoke, and every other wise dilapidated. There were none in a later fashion than thirty years since, except some figures that had been cut from tailors' show-bills. There were views of cities and edifices in Europe, of Napoleon's battles and Nelson's sea-fights, in the midst of which would be seen a gigantic, brown, hairy hand (the Hand of Destiny) pointing at the principal points of the conflict, while the old Dutchman explained. He gave a good deal of dramatic effect to his descriptions, but his accent and intonation cannot be written. He seemed to take interest and pride in his exhibition; yet when the utter and ludicrous miserability thereof made us laugh, he joined in the joke very readily. When the last picture had been shown, he caused a country boor, who stood gaping beside the machine, to put his head within it, and thrust out his tongue. The head becoming gigantic, a singular effect was produced.

The old Dutchman's exhibition being over, a great dog, apparently an elderly dog, suddenly made himself the object of notice, evidently in rivalship of the Dutchman. He had seemed to be a good-natured, quiet kind of dog, offering his head to be patted by those who were kindly disposed towards him. This great, old dog, unexpectedly, and of his own motion, began to run round after his not very long tail with the utmost eagerness; and, catching hold of it, he growled furiously at it, and still continued to circle round, growling and snarling with increasing rage, as if one half of his body were at deadly enmity with the other. Faster and faster went he, round and roundabout, growing still fiercer, till at last he ceased in a state of utter exhaustion; but no sooner had his exhibition finished than he became the same mild, quiet, sensible old dog as before; and no one could have suspected him of such nonsense as getting enraged with his own tail. He was first taught this trick by attaching a bell to the end of his tail; but he now commences entirely of his own accord, and I really believe he feels vain at the attention he excites.

It was chill and bleak on the mountain-top, and a fire was burning in the bar-room. The old Dutchman bestowed on everybody the title of "Captain," perhaps because such a title has a great chance of suiting an American.

Leaving the tavern, we drove a mile or two farther to the eastern brow of the mountain, whence we had a view, over the tops of a multitude of heights, into the intersecting valleys down which we were to plunge,—and beyond them the blue and indistinctive scene extended to the east and north for at least sixty miles. Beyond the hills it looked almost as if the blue ocean might be seen. Monadnock was visible, like a sapphire cloud against the sky. Descending, we by and by got a view of the Deerfield River, which makes a bend in its course from about north and south to about east and west, coming out from one defile among the mountains, and flowing through another

The scenery on the eastern side of the Green Mountains is incomparably more striking than on the western, where the long swells and ridges have a flatness of effect; and even Graylock heaves itself so gradually that it does not much strike the beholder. But on the eastern part, peaks one or two thousand feet high rush up on either bank of the river in ranges, thrusting out their shoulders side by side. They are almost precipitous, clothed in woods, through which the naked rock pushes itself forth to view. Sometimes the peak is bald, while the forest wraps the body of the hill, and the baldness gives it an indescribably stern effect. Sometimes the precipice rises with abruptness from the immediate side of the river; sometimes there is a cultivated valley on either side,—cultivated long, and with all the smoothness and antique rurality of a farm near cities,—this gentle picture strongly set off by the wild mountain-frame around it. Often it would seem a wonder how our road was to continue, the mountains rose so abruptly on either side, and stood, so direct a wall, across our onward course; while, looking behind, it would be an equal mystery how we had gotten thither, through the huge base of the mountain, that seemed to have reared itself erect after our passage. But, passing onward, a narrow defile would give us egress into a scene where new mountains would still appear to bar us. Our road was much of it level; but scooped out among mountains. The river was a brawling stream, shallow, and roughened by rocks; now we drove on a plane with it; now there was a sheer descent down from the roadside upon it, often unguarded by any kind of fence, except by the trees that contrived to grow on the headlong interval. Between the mountains there were gorges, that led the imagination away into new scenes of wildness. I have never driven through such romantic scenery, where there was such variety and boldness of mountain shapes as this; and though it was a broad sunny day, the mountains diversified the view with sunshine and shadow, and glory and gloom.

In Charlemont (I think), after passing a bridge, we saw a very curious rock on the shore of the river, about twenty feet from the roadside. Clambering down the bank, we found it a complete arch, hollowed out of the solid rock, and as high as the arched entrance of an ancient church, which it might be taken to be, though considerably dilapidated and weather-worn. The water flows through it, though the rock afforded standing room, beside the

127

pillars. It was really like the archway of an enchanted palace, all of which has vanished except the entrance,—now only into nothingness and empty space. We climbed to the top of the arch, in which the traces of water having eddied are very perceptible. This curiosity occurs in a wild part of the river's course, and in a solitude of mountains.

Farther down, the river becoming deeper, broader, and more placid, little boats were seen moored along it, for the convenience of crossing. Sometimes, too, the well-beaten track of wheels and hoofs passed down to its verge, then vanished, and appeared on the other side, indicating a ford. We saw one house, pretty, small, with green blinds, and much quietness in its environments, on the other side of the river, with a flat-bottomed boat for communication. It was a pleasant idea that the world was kept off by the river.

Proceeding onward, we reached Shelburne Falls. Here the river, in the distance of a few hundred yards, makes a descent of about a hundred and fifty feet over a prodigious bed of rock. Formerly it doubtless flowed unbroken over the rock, merely creating a rapid; and traces of water having raged over it are visible in portions of the rock that now lie high and dry. At present the river roars through a channel which it has worn in the stone, leaping in two or three distinct falls, and rushing downward, as from flight to flight of a broken and irregular staircase. The mist rises from the highest of these cataracts, and forms a pleasant object in the sunshine. The best view, I think, is to stand on the verge of the upper and largest fall, and look down through the whole rapid descent of the river, as it hurries, foaming, through its rock-worn path,—the rocks seeming to have been hewn away, as when mortals make a road. These falls are the largest in this State, and have a very peculiar character. It seems as if water had had more power at some former period than now, to hew and tear its passage through such an immense ledge of rock as here withstood it. In this crag, or parts of it, now far beyond the reach of the water, it has worn what are called pot-holes,—being circular hollows in the rock, where for ages stones have been whirled round and round by the eddies of the water; so that the interior of the pot is as circular and as smooth as it could have been made by art. Often the mouth of the pot is the narrowest part, the inner space being deeply scooped out. Water is contained in most of these pot-holes, sometimes so deep that a man might drown himself therein, and lie undetected at the bottom. Some of them are of a convenient size for cooking, which might be practicable by putting in hot stones.

The tavern at Shelburne Falls was about the worst I ever saw,—there being hardly anything to eat, at least nothing of the meat kind. There was a party of students from the Rensselaer school at Troy, who had spent the night there, a set of rough urchins from sixteen to twenty years old, accompanied by the wagon-driver, a short, stubbed little fellow, who walked about with great independence, thrusting his hands into his breeches-pockets, beneath his frock. The queerness was, such a figure being associated with classic youth. They were on an excursion which is yearly made from that school in search of minerals. They seemed in rather better moral habits than students used to be, but wild-spirited, rude, and unpolished, somewhat like German students, which resemblance one or two of them increased by smoking pipes. In the morning, my breakfast being set in a corner of the same room with them, I saw their breakfast-table, with a huge wash-bowl of milk in the centre, and a basin and spoon placed for each guest.

In the bar-room of this tavern were posted up written advertisements, the smoked chimney-piece being thus made to serve for a newspaper: "I have rye for sale," "I have a fine mare colt," etc. There was one quaintly expressed advertisement of a horse that had strayed or been stolen from a pasture.

The students, from year to year, have been in search of a particular rock, somewhere on the mountains in the vicinity of Shelburne Falls, which is supposed to contain some valuable ore; but they cannot find it. One man in the bar-room observed that it must be enchanted; and spoke of a tinker, during the Revolutionary War, who met with a somewhat similar instance. Roaming along the Hudson River, he came to a precipice which had some bunches of singular appearance embossed upon it. He knocked off one of the hunches, and carrying it home, or to a camp, or wherever he lived, he put it on the fire, and incited it down into clear lead. He sought for the spot again and again, but could never find it.

Mr. Leach's brother is a student at Shelburne Falls. He is about thirty-five years old, and married; and at this mature age he is studying for the ministry, and will not finish his course for two or three years. He was bred a farmer, but has sold his farm, and invested the money, and supports himself and wife by dentistry during his studies. Many of the academy students are men grown, and some, they say, well towards forty years old. Methinks this is characteristic of American life,—these rough, weather-beaten, hard-handed, farmer-bred students. In nine cases out of ten they are incapable of any effectual cultivation; for men of ripe years, if they have any pith in them, will have long ago got beyond academy or even college instruction. I suspect nothing better than a very wretched smattering is to be obtained in these country academies.

Mr. Jerkins, an instructor at Amherst, speaking of the Western mounds, expressed an opinion that they were of the same nature and origin as some small circular hills which are of very frequent occurrence here in North Adams. The burial-ground is on one of them, and there is another, on the summit of which appears a single tombstone, as if there were something natural in making these hills the repositories of the dead. A question of old H———— led to Mr. Jenkins's dissertation on this subject, to the great contentment of a large circle round the bar-room fireside on the last rainy day.

A tailor is detected by Mr. Leach, because his coat had not a single wrinkle in it. I saw him exhibiting patterns of fashions to Randall, the village tailor. Mr. Leach has much tact in finding out the professions of people. He found out a blacksmith, because his right hand was much larger than the other.

A man getting subscriptions for a religious and abolition newspaper in New York,—somewhat elderly and gray-haired, quick in his movements, hasty in his walk, with an eager, earnest stare through his spectacles, hurrying about with a pocket-book of subscriptions in his hand,—seldom speaking, and then in brief expressions,—sitting down before the stage comes, to write a list of subscribers obtained to his employers in New York. Withal, a city and business air about him, as of one accustomed to hurry through narrow alleys, and dart across thronged streets, and speak hastily to one man and another at jostling corners, though now transacting his affairs in the solitude of mountains.

An old, gray man, seemingly astray and abandoned in this wide world, sitting in the bar-room, speaking to none, nor addressed by any one. Not understanding the meaning of the supper-bell till asked to supper by word of mouth. However, he called for a glass of brandy.

A pedler, with girls' silk neckerchiefs,—or gauze,—men's silk pocket-handkerchiefs, red bandannas, and a variety of horn combs, trying to trade with the servant-girls of the house. One of them, Laura, attempts to exchange a worked vandyke, which she values at two dollars and a half; Eliza, being reproached by the pedler, "vows that she buys more of pedlers than any other person in the house."

A drove of pigs passing at dusk. They appeared not so much disposed to ramble and go astray from the line of march as in daylight, but kept together in a pretty compact body. There was a general grunting, not violent at all, but low and quiet, as if they were expressing their sentiments among themselves in a companionable way. Pigs, on a march, do not subject themselves to any leader among themselves, but pass on, higgledy-piggledy, without regard to age or sex.

September 1st.—Last evening, during a walk, Graylock and the whole of Saddleback were at first imbued with a mild, half-sunshiny tinge, then grew almost black,—a huge, dark mass lying on the back of the earth and encumbering it. Stretching up from behind the black mountain, over a third or more of the sky, there was a heavy, sombre blue heap or ledge of clouds, looking almost as solid as rocks. The volumes of which it was composed were perceptible, by translucent lines and fissures; but the mass, as a whole, seemed as solid, bulky, and ponderous in the cloud-world as the mountain was on earth. The mountain and cloud together had an indescribably stern and majestic aspect. Beneath this heavy cloud, there was a fleet or flock of light, vapory mists, flitting in middle air; and these were tinted, from the vanished sun, with the most gorgeous and living purple that can be conceived,—a fringe upon the stern blue. In the opposite quarter of the heavens, a rose-light was reflected, whence I know not, which colored the clouds around the moon, then well above the horizon, so that the nearly round and silver moon appeared strangely among roseate clouds,—sometimes half obscured by them.

A man with a smart horse, upon which the landlord makes laudatory remarks. He replies that he has "a better at home." Dressed in a brown, bright-buttoned coat, smartly cut. He immediately becomes familiar, and begins to talk of the license law, and other similar topics,—making himself at home, as one who, being much of his time upon the road, finds himself at ease at any tavern. He inquired after a stage agent, named Brigham, who formerly resided here, but now has gone to the West. He himself was probably a horse-jockey.

An old lady, stopping here over the Sabbath, waiting for to-morrow's stage for Greenfield, having been deceived by the idea that she could proceed on her journey without delay. Quiet, making herself comfortable, taken into the society of the women of the house.

September 3d.—On the slope of Bald Mountain a clearing, set in the frame of the forest on all sides,—a growth of clover upon it, which, having been mowed once this year, is now appropriated to pasturage. Stumps remaining in the ground; one tall, barkless stem of a tree standing upright, branchless, and with a shattered summit. One or two other stems lying prostrate and partly overgrown with bushes and shrubbery, some of them bearing a yellow flower,—a color which Autumn loves. The stumps and trunks fire-blackened, yet nothing about them that indicates a recent clearing, but the roughness of an old clearing, that, being removed from convenient labor, has none of the polish of the homestead. The field, with slight undulations, slopes pretty directly down. Near the lower verge, a rude sort of barn, or rather haystack roofed over, and with hay protruding and hanging out. An ox feeding, and putting up his muzzle to pull down a mouthful of hay; but seeing me, a stranger, in the upper part of the field, he remains long gazing, and finally betakes himself to feeding again. A solitary butterfly flitting to and fro, blown slightly on its course by a cool September wind,—the coolness of which begins to be tempered by a bright, glittering sun. There is dew on the grass

In front, beyond the lower spread of forest, Saddle Mountain rises, and the valleys and long, swelling hills sweep away. But the impression of this clearing is solitude, as of a forgotten land.

It is customary here to toll the bell at the death of a person, at the hour of his death, whether A. M. or P. M. Not, however, I suppose, if it happen in deep night.

"There are three times in a man's life when he is talked about,—when he is born, when he is married, and when he dies." "Yes," said Orrin S——— —, "and only one of the times has he to pay anything for it out of his own pocket." (In reference to a claim by the guests of the bar-room on the man Amasa Richardson for a treat.)

A wood-chopper, travelling the country in search of jobs at chopping. His baggage a bundle, a handkerchief, and a pair of coarse boots. His implement an axe, most keenly ground and sharpened, which I had noticed standing in a corner, and thought it would almost serve as a razor. I saw another wood-chopper sitting down on the ascent of Bald Mountain, with his axe on one side and a jug and provisions on the other, on the way to his day's toil.

The Revolutionary pensioners come out into the sunshine to make oath that they are still above ground. One, whom Mr. S——— saluted as "Uncle John," went into the bar-room, walking pretty stoutly by the aid of a long, oaken staff,—with an old, creased, broken and ashen bell-crowned hat on his head, and wearing a brown old-fashioned suit of clothes. Pretty portly, fleshy in the face, and with somewhat of a paunch, cheerful, and his senses, bodily and mental, in no very bad order, though he is now in his ninetieth year. "An old man's withered and wilted apple," quoth Uncle John, "keeps a good while." Mr. S——— says his grandfather lived to be a hundred, and that his legs became covered with moss, like the trunk of an old tree. Uncle John would smile and cackle at a little jest, and what life there was in him seemed a good-natured and comfortable one enough. He can walk two or three miles, he says, "taking it moderate." I suppose his state is that of a drowsy man but partly conscious of life,—walking as through a dim dream, but brighter at some seasons than at others. By and by he will fall quite asleep, without any trouble. Mr. S———, unbidden, gave him a glass of gin, which the old man imbibed by the warm fireside, and grew the younger for it.

September 4th.—This day an exhibition of animals in the vicinity of the village, under a pavilion of sail-cloth,—the floor being the natural grass, with here and there a rock partially protruding. A pleasant, mild shade; a strip of sunshine or a spot of glimmering brightness in some parts. Crowded,—row above row of women, on an amphitheatre of seats, on one side. In an inner pavilion an exhibition of anacondas,—four,—which the showman took, one by one, from a large box, under some blankets, and hung round his shoulders. They seemed almost torpid when first taken out, but gradually began to assume life, to stretch, to contract, twine and writhe about his neck and person, thrusting out their tongues and erecting their heads. Their weight was as much as he could bear, and they hung down almost to the ground when not contorted,—as big round as a thigh, almost,—spotted and richly variegated. Then he put them into the box again, their heads emerging and writhing forth, which the showman thrust back again. He gave a descriptive and historical account of them, and a fanciful and poetical one also. A man put his arm and head into the lion's mouth,—all the spectators looking on so attentively that a breath could not be heard. That was impressive,—its effect on a thousand persons,—more so than the thing itself.

In the evening the caravan people were at the tavern, talking of their troubles in coming over the mountain,—the overturn of a cage containing two leopards and a hyena. They are a rough, ignorant set of men, apparently incapable of taking any particular enjoyment from the life of variety and adventure which they lead. There was the man who put his head into the lion's mouth, and, I suppose, the man about whom the anacondas twined, talking about their suppers, and blustering for hot meat, and calling for something to drink, without anything of the wild dignity of men familiar with the nobility of nature.

A character of a desperate young man, who employs high courage and strong faculties in this sort of dangers, and wastes his talents in wild riot, addressing the audience as a snake-man,—keeping the ring while the monkey rides the pony,—singing negro and other songs.

The country boors were continually getting within the barriers, and venturing too near the cages. The great lion lay with his fore paws extended, and a calm, majestic, but awful countenance. He looked on the people as if he had seen many such concourses. The hyena was the most ugly and dangerous looking beast, full of spite, and on ill terms with all nature, looking a good deal like a hog with the devil in him, the ridge of hair along his back bristling. He was in the cage with a leopard and a panther, and the latter seemed continually on the point of laying his paw on the hyena, who snarled, and showed his teeth. It is strange, though, to see how these wild beasts acknowledge and practise a degree of mutual forbearance, and of obedience to man, with their wild nature yet in them. The great white bear seemed in distress from the heat, moving his head and body in a peculiar, fantastic way, and eagerly drinking water when given it. He was thin and lank.

The caravan men were so sleepy, Orrin S——— says, that he could hardly wake them in the morning. They turned over on their faces to show him.

Coming out of the caravansary, there were the mountains, in the quiet sunset, and many men drunk, swearing, and fighting. Shanties with liquor for sale.

The elephant lodged in the barn.

September 5th.—I took a walk of three miles from the village, which brought me into Vermont. The line runs athwart a bridge,—a rude bridge, which crosses a mountain stream. The stream runs deep at the bottom of a gorge, plashing downward, with rapids and pools, and bestrewn with large rocks, deep and shady, not to be reached by the sun except in its meridian, as well on account of the depth of the gorge as of the arch of wilderness trees above it. There was a stumpy clearing beyond the bridge, where some men were building a house. I went to them, and inquired if I were in Massachusetts or Vermont, and asked for some water. Whereupon they showed great hospitality, and the master-workman went to the spring, and brought delicious water in a tin basin, and produced another jug containing "new rum, and very good; and rum does nobody any harm if they make a good use of it," quoth he. I invited them to call on me at the hotel, if they should cone to the village within two or three days. Then I took my way back through the forest, for this is a by-road, and is, much of its course, a sequestrated and wild one, with an unseen torrent roaring at an unseen depth, along the roadside.

My walk forth had been an almost continued ascent, and, returning, I had an excellent view of Graylock and the adjacent mountains, at such a distance that they were all brought into one group, and comprehended at one view, as belonging to the same company,—all mighty, with a mightier chief. As I drew nearer home, they separated, and the unity of effect was lost. The more distant then disappeared behind the nearer ones, and finally Graylock itself was lost behind the hill which immediately shuts in the village. There was a warm, autumnal haze, which, I think, seemed to throw the mountains farther off, and both to enlarge and soften them.

To imagine the gorges and deep hollows in among the group of mountains,— their huge shoulders and protrusions.

"They were just beginning to pitch over the mountains, as I came along," —stage-driver's expression about the caravan.

A fantastic figure of a village coxcomb, striding through the bar-room, and standing with folded arms to survey the caravan men. There is much exaggeration and rattle-brain about this fellow.

A mad girl leaped from the top of a tremendous precipice in Pownall, hundreds of feet high, if the tale be true, and, being buoyed up by her clothes, came safely to the bottom.

Inquiries about the coming of the caravan, and whether the elephant had got to town, and reports that he had.

A smart, plump, crimson-faced gentleman, with a travelling-portmanteau of peculiar neatness and convenience. He criticises the road over the mountain, having come in the Greenfield stage; perhaps an engineer.

Bears still inhabit Saddleback and the neighboring mountains and forests. Six were taken in Pownall last year, and two hundred foxes. Sometimes they appear on the hills, in close proximity to this village.

September 7th.—Mr. Leach and I took a walk by moonlight last evening, on the road that leads over the mountain. Remote from houses, far up on the hillside, we found a lime-kiln, burning near the road; and, approaching it, a watcher started from the ground, where he had been lying at his length. There are several of these lime-kilns in this vicinity. They are circular, built with stones, like a round tower, eighteen or twenty feet high, having a hillock heaped around in a great portion of their circumference, so that the marble may be brought and thrown in by cart-loads at the top. At the bottom there is a doorway, large enough to admit a man in a stooping posture. Thus an edifice of great solidity is constructed, which will endure for centuries, unless needless pains are taken to tear it down. There is one on the hillside, close to the village, wherein weeds grow at the bottom, and grass and shrubs too are rooted in the interstices of the stones, and its low doorway has a dungeon-like aspect, and we look down from the top as into a roofless tower. It apparently has not been used for many years, and the lime and weather-stained fragments of marble are scattered about.

But in the one we saw last night a hard-wood fire was burning merrily, beneath the superincumbent marble,—the kiln being heaped full; and shortly after we came, the man (a dark, black-bearded figure, in shirt-sleeves) opened the iron door, through the chinks of which the fire was gleaming, and thrust in huge logs of wood, and stirred the immense coals with a long pole, and showed us the glowing limestone,—the lower layer of it. The heat of the fire was powerful, at the distance of several yards from the open door. He talked very sensibly with us, being doubtless glad to have two visitors to vary his solitary night-watch; for it would not do for him to fall asleep, since the fire should be refreshed as often as every twenty minutes. We ascended the hillock to the top of the kiln, and the marble was red-hot, and burning with a bluish, lambent flame, quivering up, sometimes nearly a yard high, and resembling the flame of anthracite coal, only, the marble being in large fragments, the flame was higher. The kiln was perhaps six or eight feet across.

Four hundred bushels of marble were then in a state of combustion. The expense of converting this quantity into lime is about fifty dollars, and it sells for twenty-five cents per bushel at the kiln. We asked the man whether he would run across the top of the intensely burning kiln, barefooted, for a thousand dollars; and he said he would for ten. He told us that the lime had been burning forty-eight hours, and would be finished in thirty-six more. He liked the business of watching it better by night than by day; because the days were often hot, but such a mild and beautiful night as the last was just right. Here a poet might make verses with moonlight in them, and a gleam of fierce firelight flickering through. It is a shame to use this brilliant, white, almost transparent marble in this way. A man said of it, the other day, that into some pieces of it, when polished, one could see a good distance; and he instanced a certain gravestone.

Visited the cave. A large portion of it, where water trickles and falls, is perfectly white. The walls present a specimen of how Nature packs the stone, crowding huge masses, as it were, into chinks and fissures, and here we see it in the perpendicular or horizontal layers, as Nature laid it.

September 9th.—A walk yesterday forenoon through the Notch, formed between Saddle Mountain and another adjacent one. This Notch is otherwise called the Bellowspipe, being a long and narrow valley, with a steep wall on either side. The walls are very high, and the fallen timbers lie strewed adown the precipitous descent. The valley gradually descends from the narrowest part of the Notch, and a stream of water flows through the midst of it, which, farther onward in its course, turns a mill. The valley is cultivated, there being two or three farm-houses towards the northern end, and extensive fields of grass beyond, where stand the hay-mows of last year, with the hay cut away regularly around their bases. All the more distant portion of the valley is lonesome in the extreme; and on the hither side of the narrowest part the land is uncultivated, partly overgrown with forest, partly used as sheep-pastures, for which purpose it is not nearly so barren as sheep-pastures usually are. On the right, facing southward, rises Graylock, all beshagged with forest and with headlong precipices of rock appearing among the black pines Southward there is a most extensive view of the valley, in which Saddlebacl and its companion mountains are crouched,—wide and far,—a broad, misty valley, fenced in by a mountain wall, and with villages scattered along it, and miles of forest, which appear but as patches scattered here and there upon the landscape. The descent from the Notch southward is much more abrupt than on the other side. A stream flows down through it; and along much of its course it has washed away all the earth from a ledge of rock, and then formed a descending pavement, smooth and regular, which the scanty flow of water scarcely suffices to moisten at this period, though a heavy rain, probably, would send down a torrent, raging, roaring, and foaming. I descended along the course of the stream, and sometimes on the rocky path of it, and, turning off towards the south village, followed a cattle-path till I came to a cottage.

A horse was standing saddled near the door, but I did not see the rider. I knocked, and an elderly woman, of very pleasing and intelligent aspect, came at the summons, and gave me directions how to get to the south village through an orchard and "across lots," which would bring me into the road near the Quaker meeting-house, with gravestones round it. While she talked, a young woman came into the pantry from the kitchen, with a dirty little brat, whose squalls I had heard all along; the reason of his outcry being that his mother was washing him,—a very unusual process, if I may judge by his looks. I asked the old lady for some water, and she gave me, I think, the most delicious I ever tasted. These mountaineers ought certainly to be temperance people; for their mountain springs supply them with a liquor of which the cities and the low countries can have no conception. Pure, fresh, almost sparkling, exhilarating,—such water as Adam and Eve drank.

I passed the south village on a by-road, without entering it, and was taken up by the stage from Pittsfield a mile or two this side of it. Platt, the driver, a friend of mine, talked familiarly about many matters, intermixing his talk with remarks on his team and addresses to the beasts composing it, who were three mares, and a horse on the near wheel,—all bays. The horse he pronounced "a dreadful nice horse to go; but if he could shirk off the work upon the others, he would,"—which unfairness Platt corrected by timely strokes of the whip whenever the horse's traces were not tightened. One of the mares wished to go faster, hearing another horse tramp behind her; "and nothing made her so mad," quoth Platt, "as to be held in when she wanted to go." The near leader started. "O the little devil," said he, "how skittish she is!" Another stumbled, and Platt bantered her thereupon. Then he told of foundering through snow-drifts in winter, and carrying the mail on his back—four miles from Bennington. And thus we jogged on, and got to "mine inn" just as the dinner-bell was ringing.

Pig-drover, with two hundred pigs. They are much more easily driven on rainy days than on fair ones. One of his pigs, a large one, particularly troublesome as to running off the road towards every object, and leading the drove. Thirteen miles about a day's journey, in the course of which the drover has to travel about thirty.

They have a dog, who runs to and fro indefatigably, barking at those who straggle on the flanks of the line of march, then scampering to the other side and barking there, and sometimes having quite an affair of barking and surly grunting with some refractory pig, who has found something to munch, and refuses to quit it. The pigs are fed on corn at their halts. The drove has some ultimate market, and individuals are peddled out on the march. Some die.

Merino sheep (which are much raised in Berkshire) are good for hardly anything to eat,—a fair-sized quarter dwindling down to almost nothing in the process of roasting.

The tavern-keeper in Stockbridge, an elderly bachelor,—a dusty, black-dressed, antiquated figure, with a white neckcloth setting off a dim, yellow complexion, looking like one of the old wax-figures of ministers in a corner of the New England Museum. He did not seem old, but like a middle-aged man, who had been preserved in some dark and cobwebby corner for a great while. He is asthmatic.

In Connecticut, and also sometimes in Berkshire, the villages are situated on the most elevated ground that can be found, so that they are visible for miles around. Litchfield is a remarkable instance, occupying a high plain, without the least shelter from the winds, and with almost as wide an expanse of view as from a mountain-top. The streets are very wide,—two or three hundred feet, at least,—with wide, green margins, and sometimes there is a wide green space between two road tracks. Nothing can be neater than the churches and houses. The graveyard is on the slope, and at the foot of a swell, filled with old and new gravestones, some of red freestone, some of gray granite, most of them of white marble, and one of cast-iron with an inscription of raised letters. There was one of the date of about 1776, on which was represented the third-length, has-relief portrait of a gentleman in a wig and other costume of that day; and as a framework about this portrait was wreathed a garland of vine-leaves and heavy clusters of grapes. The deceased should have been a jolly bottleman; but the epitaph indicated nothing of the kind.

In a remote part of the graveyard,—remote from the main body of dead people,—I noticed a humble, mossy stone, on which I traced out "To the memory of Julia Africa, servant of Rev." somebody. There were also the half-obliterated traces of other graves, without any monuments, in the vicinity of this one. Doubtless the slaves here mingled their dark clay with the earth.

At Litchfield there is a doctor who undertakes to cure deformed people,— and humpbacked, lame, and otherwise defective folk go there. Besides these, there were many ladies and others boarding there, for the benefit of the air, I suppose.

At Canaan, Connecticut, before the tavern, there is a doorstep, two or three paces large in each of its dimensions; and on this is inscribed the date when the builder of the house came to the town,—namely, 1731. The house was built in 1751. Then follows the age and death of the patriarch (at over ninety) and his wife, and the births of, I think, eleven sons and daughters. It would seem as if they were buried underneath; and many people take that idea. It is odd to put a family record in a spot where it is sure to be trampled underfoot.

At Springfield, a blind man, who came in the stage,—elderly,—sitting in the reading-room, and, as soon as seated, feeling all around him with his cane, so as to find out his locality, and know where he may spit with safety! The cautious and scientific air with which he measures his distances. Then

141

he sits still and silent a long while,—then inquires the hour,—then says, "I should like to go to bed." Nobody of the house being near, he receives no answer, and repeats impatiently, "I'll go to bed." One would suppose, that, conscious of his dependent condition, he would have learned a different sort of manner; but probably he has lived where he could command attention.

Two travellers, eating bread and cheese of their own in the bar-room at Stockbridge, and drinking water out of a tumbler borrowed from the landlord. Eating immensely, and, when satisfied, putting the relics in their trunk, and rubbing down the table.

Sample ears of various kinds of corn hanging over the looking-glass or in the bars of taverns. Four ears on a stalk (good ones) are considered a heavy harvest.

A withered, yellow, sodden, dead-alive looking woman,—an opium-eater. A deaf man, with a great fancy for conversation, so that his interlocutor is compelled to halloo and bawl over the rumbling of the coach, amid which he hears best. The sharp tones of a woman's voice appear to pierce his dull organs much better than a masculine voice. The impossibility of saying anything but commonplace matters to a deaf man, of expressing any delicacy of thought in a raised tone, of giving utterance to fine feelings in a bawl. This man's deafness seemed to have made his mind and feelings uncommonly coarse; for, after the opium-eater had renewed an old acquaintance with him, almost the first question he asked, in his raised voice, was, "Do you eat opium now?"

At Hartford, the keeper of a temperance hotel reading a Hebrew Bible in the bar by means of a lexicon and an English version.

A negro, respectably dressed, and well-mounted on horseback, travelling on his own hook, calling for oats, and drinking a glass of brandy-and-water at the bar, like any other Christian. A young man from Wisconsin said, "I wish I had a thousand such fellows in Alabama." It made a strange impression on me,—the negro was really so human!—and to talk of owning a thousand like him!

Left North Adams September 11th. Reached home September 24th, 1838.

October 24th.—View from a chamber of the Tremont of the brick edifice, opposite, on the other side of Beacon Street. At one of the lower windows, a woman at work; at one above, a lady hemming a ruff or some such ladylike thing. She is pretty, young, and married; for a little boy comes to her knees, and she parts his hair, and caresses him in a motherly way. A note on colored paper is brought her; and she reads it, and puts it in her bosom. At another window, at some depth within the apartment, a gentleman in a dressing-gown, reading, and rocking in an easy-chair, etc., etc., etc. A rainy day, and people passing with umbrellas disconsolately between the spectator and these various scenes of indoor occupation and comfort. With this sketch might be mingled and worked up some story that was going on within the chamber where the spectator was situated.

All the dead that had ever been drowned in a certain lake to arise.

The history of a small lake from the first, till it was drained.

An autumnal feature,—boys had swept together the fallen leaves from the elms along the street in one huge pile, and had made a hollow, nest-shaped, in this pile, in which three or four of them lay curled, like young birds.

A tombstone-maker, whom Miss B——y knew, used to cut cherubs on the top of the tombstones, and had the art of carving the cherubs' faces in the likeness of the deceased.

A child of Rev. E. P——— was threatened with total blindness. A week after the father had been informed of this, the child died; and, in the mean while, his feelings had become so much the more interested in the child, from its threatened blindness, that it was infinitely harder to give it up. Had he not been aware of it till after the child's death, it would probably have been a consolation.

Singular character of a gentleman (H. H———, Esq.) living in retirement in Boston,—esteemed a man of nicest honor, and his seclusion attributed to wounded feelings on account of the failure of his firm in business. Yet it was discovered that this man had been the mover of intrigues by which men in business had been ruined, and their property absorbed, none knew how or by whom; love-affairs had been broken off, and much other mischief done; and for years he was not in the least suspected. He died suddenly, soon after suspicion fell upon him. Probably it was the love of management, of having an influence on affairs, that produced these phenomena.

Character of a man who, in himself and his external circumstances, shall be equally and totally false: his fortune resting on baseless credit,— his patriotism assumed,—his domestic affections, his honor and honesty, all a sham. His own misery in the midst of it,—it making the whole universe, heaven and earth alike, all unsubstantial mockery to him.

Dr. Johnson's penance in Uttoxeter Market. A man who does penance in what might appear to lookers-on the most glorious and triumphal circumstance of his life. Each circumstance of the career of an apparently successful man to be a penance and torture to him on account of some fundamental error in early life.

A person to catch fire-flies, and try to kindle his household fire with them. It would be symbolical of something.

Thanksgiving at the Worcester Lunatic Asylum. A ball and dance of the inmates in the evening,—a furious lunatic dancing with the principal's wife. Thanksgiving in an almshouse might make a better sketch.

The house on the eastern corner of North and Essex Streets [Salem], supposed to have been built about 1640, had, say sixty years later, a brick turret erected, wherein one of the ancestors of the present occupants used to practise alchemy. He was the operative of a scientific person in Boston, the director. There have been other alchemists of old in this town,—one who kept his fire burning seven weeks, and then lost the elixir by letting it go out.

An ancient wineglass (Miss Ingersol's), long-stalked, with a small, cup-like bowl, round which is wreathed a branch of grape-vine, with a rich cluster of grapes, and leaves spread out. There is also some kind of a bird flying. The whole is excellently cut or engraved.

In the Duke of Buckingham's comedy "The Chances," Don Frederic says of Don John (they are two noble Spanish gentlemen), "One bed contains us ever."

A person, while awake and in the business of life, to think highly of another, and place perfect confidence in him, but to be troubled with dreams in which this seeming friend appears to act the part of a most deadly enemy. Finally it is discovered that the dream-character is the true one. The explanation would be—the soul's instinctive perception.

Pandora's box for a child's story.

Moonlight is sculpture; sunlight is painting.

"A person to look back on a long life ill-spent, and to picture forth a beautiful life which he would live, if he could be permitted to begin his life over again. Finally to discover that he had only been dreaming of old age,—that he was really young, and could live such a life as he had pictured."

A newspaper, purporting to be published in a family, and satirizing the political and general world by advertisements, remarks on domestic affairs,—advertisement of a lady's lost thimble, etc.

L. H———. She was unwilling to die, because she had no friends to meet her in the other world. Her little son F. being very ill, on his recovery she confessed a feeling of disappointment, having supposed that he would have gone before, and welcomed her into heaven!

H. L. C——— heard from a French Canadian a story of a young couple in Acadie. On their marriage day, all the men of the Province were summoned to assemble in the church to hear a proclamation. When assembled, they were all seized and shipped off to be distributed through New England,— among them the new bridegroom. His bride set off in search of him,— wandered about New England all her lifetime, and at last, when she was old, she found her bridegroom on his deathbed. The shock was so great that it killed her likewise.

January 4th, 1839.—When scattered clouds are resting on the bosoms of hills, it seems as if one might climb into the heavenly region, earth being so intermixed, with sky, and gradually transformed into it.

A stranger, dying, is buried; and after many years two strangers come in search of his grave, and open it.

The strange sensation of a person who feels himself an object of deep interest, and close observation, and various construction of all his actions, by another person.

Letters in the shape of figures of men, etc. At a distance, the words composed by the letters are alone distinguishable. Close at hand, the figures alone are seen, and not distinguished as letters. Thus things may have a positive, a relative, and a composite meaning, according to the point of view.

"Passing along the street, all muddy with puddles, and suddenly seeing the sky reflected in these puddles in such a way as quite to conceal the foulness of the street."

A young man in search of happiness,—to be personified by a figure whom he expects to meet in a crowd, and is to be recognized by certain signs. All these signs are given by a figure in various garbs and actions, but he does not recognize that this is the sought-for person till too late.

If cities were built by the sound of music, then some edifices would appear to be constructed by grave, solemn tones,—others to have danced forth to light, fantastic airs.

Familiar spirits, according to Lilly, used to be worn in rings, watches, sword-hilts. Thumb-rings were set with jewels of extraordinary size.

A very fanciful person, when dead, to have his burial in a cloud.

"A story there passeth of an Indian king that sent unto Alexander a fair woman, fed with aconite and other poisons, with this intent complexionally to destroy him!"—Sir T. Browne.

Dialogues of the unborn, like dialogues of the dead,—or between two young children.

A mortal symptom for a person being to lose his own aspect and to take the family lineaments, which were hidden deep in the healthful visage. Perhaps a seeker might thus recognize the man he had sought, after long intercourse with him unknowingly.

Some moderns to build a fire on Ararat with the remnants of the ark.

Two little boats of cork, with a magnet in one and steel in the other.

To have ice in one's blood.

To make a story of all strange and impossible things,—as the Salamander, the Phoenix.

The semblance of a human face to be formed on the side of a mountain, or in the fracture of a small stone, by a lusus naturae. The face is an object of curiosity for years or centuries, and by and by a boy is born, whose features gradually assume the aspect of that portrait. At some critical juncture, the resemblance is found to be perfect. A prophecy may be connected.

A person to be the death of his beloved in trying to raise her to more than mortal perfection; yet this should be a comfort to him for having aimed so highly and holily.

1840.—A man, unknown, conscious of temptation to secret crimes, puts up a note in church, desiring the prayers of the congregation for one so tempted.

Some most secret thing, valued and honored between lovers, to be hung up in public places, and made the subject of remark by the city,—remarks, sneers, and laughter.

To make a story out of a scarecrow, giving it odd attributes. From different points of view, it should appear to change,—now an old man, now an old woman,—a gunner, a farmer, or the Old Nick.

A ground-sparrow's nest in the slope of a bank, brought to view by mowing the grass, but still sheltered and comfortably hidden by a blackberry-vine trailing over it. At first, four brown-speckled eggs,— then two little bare young ones, which, on the slightest noise, lift their heads, and open wide mouths for food,—immediately dropping their heads, after a broad gape. The action looks as if they were making a most earnest, agonized petition. In another egg, as in a coffin, I could discern the quiet, death-like form of the little bird. The whole thing had something awful and mysterious in it.

A coroner's inquest on a murdered man,—the gathering of the jury to be described, and the characters of the members,—some with secret guilt upon their souls.

To represent a man as spending life and the intensest labor in the accomplishment of some mechanical trifle,—as in making a miniature coach to be drawn by fleas, or a dinner-service to be put into a cherry-stone.

A bonfire to be made of the gallows and of all symbols of evil.

The love of posterity is a consequence of the necessity of death. If a man were sure of living forever here, he would not care about his offspring.

The device of a sun-dial for a monument over a grave, with some suitable motto.

A man with the right perception of things,—a feeling within him of what is true and what is false. It might be symbolized by the talisman with which, in fairy tales, an adventurer was enabled to distinguish enchantments from realities.

A phantom of the old royal governors, or some such shadowy pageant, on the night of the evacuation of Boston by the British.

———— taking my likeness, I said that such changes would come over my face that she would not know me when we met again in heaven. "See if I do not!" said she, smiling. There was the most peculiar and beautiful humor in the point itself, and in her manner, that can be imagined.

Little F. H———— used to look into E———'s mouth to see where her smiles came from.

"There is no Measure for Measure to my affections. If the earth fails me, I can die, and go to GOD," said ————.

Selfishness is one of the qualities apt to inspire love. This might be thought out at great length.

Boston, July 3d, 1839.—I do not mean to imply that I am unhappy or discontented, for this is not the case. My life only is a burden in the same way that it is to every toilsome man; and mine is a healthy weariness, such as needs only a night's sleep to remove it. But from henceforth forever I shall be entitled to call the sons of toil my brethren, and shall know how to sympathize with them, seeing that I likewise have risen at the dawn, and borne the fervor of the midday sun, nor turned my heavy footsteps homeward till eventide. Years hence, perhaps, the experience that my heart is acquiring now will flow out in truth and wisdom.

August 27th.—I have been stationed all day at the end of Long Wharf, and I rather think that I had the most eligible situation of anybody in Boston. I was aware that it must be intensely hot in the midst of the city; but there was only a short space of uncomfortable heat in my region, half-way towards the centre of the harbor; and almost all the time there was a pure and delightful breeze, fluttering and palpitating, sometimes shyly kissing my brow, then dying away, and then rushing upon me in livelier sport, so that I was fain to settle my straw hat more tightly upon my head. Late in the afternoon, there was a sunny shower, which came down so like a benediction that it seemed ungrateful to take shelter in the cabin or to put up an umbrella. Then there was a rainbow, or a large segment of one, so exceedingly brilliant and of such long endurance that I almost fancied it was stained into the sky, and would continue there permanently. And there were clouds floating all about,— great clouds and small, of all glorious and lovely hues (save that imperial crimson which was revealed to our united gaze),—so glorious indeed, and so lovely, that I had a fantasy of heaven's being broken into fleecy fragments and dispersed through space, with its blest inhabitants dwelling blissfully upon those scattered islands.

February 7th, 1840.—What beautiful weather this is!—beautiful, at least, so far as sun, sky, and atmosphere are concerned, though a poor, wingless biped is sometimes constrained to wish that he could raise himself a little above the earth. How much mud and mire, how many pools of unclean water, how many slippery footsteps, and perchance heavy tumbles, might be avoided, if we could tread but six inches above the crust of this world. Physically we cannot do this; our bodies cannot; but it seems to me that our hearts and minds may keep themselves above moral mud-puddles and other discomforts of the soul's pathway.

February 11th.—I have been measuring coal all day, on board of a black little British schooner, in a dismal dock at the north end of the city. Most of the time I paced the deck to keep myself warm; for the wind (northeast, I believe) blew up through the dock, as if it had been the pipe of a pair of bellows. The vessel lying deep between two wharfs, there was no more delightful prospect, on the right hand and on the left, than the posts and timbers, half immersed in the water, and covered with ice, which the rising and falling of successive tides had left upon them, so that they looked like immense icicles. Across the water, however, not more than half a mile off, appeared the Bunker Hill Monument; and what interested me considerably more, a church-steeple, with the dial of a clock upon it, whereby I was enabled to measure the march of the weary hours. Sometimes I descended into the dirty little cabin of the schooner, and warmed myself by a red-hot stove, among biscuit-barrels, pots and kettles, sea-chests, and innumerable lumber of all sorts,—my olfactories, meanwhile, being greatly refreshed by the odor of a pipe, which the captain, or some one of his crew, was smoking. But at last came the sunset, with delicate clouds, and a purple light upon the islands; and I blessed it, because it was the signal of my release.

February 12th.—All day long again have I been engaged in a very black business,—as black as a coal; and, though my face and hands have undergone a thorough purification, I feel not altogether fit to hold communion with doves. Methinks my profession is somewhat akin to that of a chimney-sweeper; but the latter has the advantage over me, because, after climbing up through the darksome flue of the chimney, he emerges into the midst of the golden air, and sings out his melodies far over the heads of the whole tribe of weary earth-plodders. My toil to-day has been cold and dull enough nevertheless, I was neither cold nor dull.

March 15th.—I pray that in one year more I may find some way of escaping from this unblest Custom-House; for it is a very grievous thraldom. I do detest all offices,—all, at least, that are held on a political tenure. And I want nothing to do with politicians. Their hearts wither away, and die out of their bodies. Their consciences are turned to india-rubber, or to some substance as black as that, and which will stretch as much. One thing, if no more, I have gained by my custom-house experience,—to know a politician. It is a knowledge which no previous thought or power of sympathy could have taught me, because the animal, or the machine rather, is not in nature.

March 23d.—I do think that it is the doom laid upon me, of murdering so many of the brightest hours of the day at the Custom-House, that makes such havoc with my wits, for here I am again trying to write worthily, ... yet with a sense as if all the noblest part of man had been left out of my composition, or had decayed out of it since my nature was given to my own keeping. . . . Never comes any bird of Paradise into that dismal region. A salt or even a coal ship is ten million times preferable; for there the sky is above me, and the fresh breeze around me, and my thoughts, having hardly anything to do with my occupation, are as free as air.

Nevertheless, you are not to fancy that the above paragraph gives a correct idea of my mental and spiritual state. . . . It is only once in a while that the image and desire of a better and happier life makes me feel the iron of my chain; for, after all, a human spirit may find no insufficiency of food fit for it, even in the Custom-House. And, with such materials as these, I do think and feel and learn things that are worth knowing, and which I should not know unless I had learned them there, so that the present portion of my life shall not be quite left out of the sum of my real existence. . . . It is good for me, on many accounts, that my life has had this passage in it. I know much more than I did a year ago. I have a stronger sense of power to act as a man among men. I have gained worldly wisdom, and wisdom also that is not altogether of this world. And, when I quit this earthly cavern where I am now buried, nothing will cling to me that ought to be left behind. Men will not perceive, I trust, by my look, or the tenor of my thoughts and feelings, that I have been a custom-house officer.

April 7th.—It appears to me to have been the most uncomfortable day that ever was inflicted on poor mortals. . . . Besides the bleak, unkindly air, I have been plagued by two sets of coal-shovellers at the same time, and have been obliged to keep two separate tallies simultaneously. But I was conscious that all this was merely a vision and a fantasy, and that, in reality, I was not half frozen by the bitter blast, nor tormented by those grimy coal-beavers, but that I was basking quietly in the sunshine of eternity. . . . Any sort of bodily and earthly torment may serve to make us sensible that we have a soul that is not within the jurisdiction of such shadowy demons,—it separates the immortal within us from the mortal. But the wind has blown my brains into such confusion that I cannot philosophize now.

April 19th.—. . . . What a beautiful day was yesterday! My spirit rebelled against being confined in my darksome dungeon at the Custom-House. It seemed a sin,—a murder of the joyful young day,—a quenching of the sunshine. Nevertheless, there I was kept a prisoner till it was too late to fling myself on a gentle wind, and be blown away into the country. . . . When I shall be again free, I will enjoy all things with the fresh simplicity of a child of five years old. I shall grow young again, made all over anew. I will go forth and stand in a summer shower, and all the worldly dust that has collected on me shall be washed away at once, and my heart will be like a bank of fresh flowers for the weary to rest upon. . . .

6 P. M.—I went out to walk about an hour ago, and found it very pleasant, though there was a somewhat cool wind. I went round and across the Common, and stood on the highest point of it, where I could see miles and miles into the country. Blessed be God for this green tract, and the view which it affords, whereby we poor citizens may be put in mind, sometimes, that all his earth is not composed of blocks of brick houses, and of stone or wooden pavements. Blessed be God for the sky too, though the smoke of the city may somewhat change its aspect,—but still it is better than if each street were covered over with a roof. There were a good many people walking on the mall,—mechanics apparently, and shopkeepers' clerks, with their wives and boys were rolling on the grass, and I would have liked to lie down and roll too.

April 30th.—. . . . I arose this morning feeling more elastic than I have throughout the winter; for the breathing of the ocean air has wrought a very beneficial effect. . . . What a beautiful, most beautiful afternoon this has been! It was a real happiness to live. If I had been merely a vegetable,—a hawthorn-bush, for instance,— I must have been happy in such an air and sunshine; but, having a mind and a soul, ... I enjoyed somewhat more than mere vegetable happiness. . . . The footsteps of May can be traced upon the islands in the harbor, and I have been watching the tints of green upon them gradually deepening, till now they are almost as beautiful as they ever can be.

May 19th.—. . . . Lights and shadows are continually flitting across my inward sky, and I know neither whence they come nor whither they go; nor do I inquire too closely into them. It is dangerous to look too minutely into such phenomena. It is apt to create a substance where at first there was a mere shadow. . . . If at any time there should seem to be an expression unintelligible from one soul to another, it is best not to strive to interpret it in earthly language, but wait for the soul to make itself understood; and, were we to wait a thousand years, we need deem it no more time than we can spare. . . . It is not that I have any love of mystery, but because I abhor it, and because I have often felt that words may be a thick and darksome veil of mystery between the soul and the truth which it seeks. Wretched were we, indeed, if we had no better means of communicating ourselves, no fairer garb in which to array our essential being, than these poor rags and tatters of Babel. Yet words are not without their use even for purposes of explanation,—but merely for explaining outward acts and all sorts of external things, leaving the soul's life and action to explain itself in its own way.

What a misty disquisition I have scribbled! I would not read it over for sixpence.

May 29th.—Rejoice with me, for I am free from a load of coal which has been pressing upon my shoulders throughout all the hot weather. I am convinced that Christian's burden consisted of coal; and no wonder he felt so much relieved, when it fell off and rolled into the sepulchre. His load, however, at the utmost, could not have been more than a few bushels, whereas mine was exactly one hundred and thirty-five chaldrons and seven tubs.

May 30th.—. . . . On board my salt-vessels and colliers there are many things happening, many pictures which, in future years, when I am again busy at the loom of fiction, I could weave in; but my fancy is rendered so torpid by my ungenial way of life that I cannot sketch off the scenes and portraits that interest me, and I am forced to trust them to my memory, with the hope of recalling them at some more favorable period. For these three or four days I have been observing a little Mediterranean boy from Malaga, not more than ten or eleven years old, but who is already a citizen of the world, and seems to be just as gay and contented on the deck of a Yankee coal-vessel as he could be while playing beside his mother's door. It is really touching to see how free and happy he is,—how the little fellow takes the whole wide world for his home, and all mankind for his family. He talks Spanish,—at least that is his native tongue; but he is also very intelligible in English, and perhaps he likewise has smatterings of the speech of other countries, whither the winds may have wafted this little sea-bird. He is a Catholic; and yesterday being Friday he caught some fish and fried them for his dinner in sweet-oil, and really they looked so delicate that I almost wished he would invite me to partake. Every once in a while he undresses himself and leaps overboard, plunging down beneath the waves as if the sea were as native to him as the earth. Then he runs up the rigging of the vessel as if he meant to fly away through the air. I must remember this little boy, and perhaps I may make something more beautiful of him than these rough and imperfect touches would promise.

June 11th.—. . . . I could wish that the east-wind would blow every day from ten o'clock till five; for there is great refreshment in it to us poor mortals that toil beneath the sun. We must not think too unkindly even of the east-wind. It is not, perhaps, a wind to be loved, even in its benignest moods; but there are seasons when I delight to feel its breath upon my cheek, though it be never advisable to throw open my bosom and take it into my heart, as I would its gentle sisters of the south and west. To-day, if I had been on the wharves, the slight chill of an east-wind would have been a blessing, like the chill of death to a world-weary man.

. . . . But this has been one of the idlest days that I ever spent in Boston.
. . . In the morning, soon after breakfast, I went to the Athenaeum gallery,
and, during the hour or two that I stayed, not a single visitor came in. Some
people were putting up paintings in one division of the room; but I had the
other all to myself. There are two pictures there by our friend Sarah Clarke,—
scenes in Kentucky.

From the picture-gallery I went to the reading-rooms of the Athenaeum,
and there read the magazines till nearly twelve; thence to the Custom-House,
and soon afterwards to dinner with Colonel Hall; then back to the Custom-
House, but only for a little while. There was nothing in the world to do, and
so at two o'clock I cane home and lay down, with the Faerie Queene in my
hand.

August 21st.—Last night I slept like a child of five years old, and had no
dreams at all,—unless just before it was time to rise, and I have forgotten what
those dreams were. After I was fairly awake this morning, I felt very bright
and airy, and was glad that I had been compelled to snatch two additional
hours of existence from annihilation. The sun's disk was but half above the
ocean's verge when I ascended the ship's side. These early morning hours are
very lightsome and quiet. Almost the whole day I have been in the shade,
reclining on a pile of sails, so that the life and spirit are not entirely worn out
of me. . . . The wind has been east this afternoon,—perhaps in the forenoon,
too,—and I could not help feeling refreshed, when the gentle chill of its
breath stole over my cheek. I would fain abominate the east-wind, ... but it
persists in doing me kindly offices now and then. What a perverse wind it is!
Its refreshment is but another mode of torment.

Salem, Oct. 4th. Union Street [Family Mansion]—. . . . Here I sit in
my old accustomed chamber, where I used to sit in days gone by. . . . Here
I have written many tales, many that have been burned to ashes, many that
doubtless deserved the same fate. This claims to be called a haunted chamber,
for thousands upon thousands of visions have appeared to me in it; and
some few of them have become visible to the world. If ever I should have a
biographer, he ought to make great mention of this chamber in my memoirs,
because so much of my lonely youth was wasted here, and here my mind and

character were formed; and here I have been glad and hopeful, and here I have been despondent. And here I sat a long, long time, waiting patiently for the world to know me, and sometimes wondering why it did not know me sooner, or whether it would ever know me at all,— at least, till I were in my grave. And sometimes it seemed as if I were already in the grave, with only life enough to be chilled and benumbed. But oftener I was happy,—at least, as happy as I then knew how to be, or was aware of the possibility of being. By and by, the world found me out in my lonely chamber, and called me forth,—not, indeed, with a loud roar of acclamation, but rather with a still, small voice,—and forth I went, but found nothing in the world that I thought preferable to my old solitude till now. . . . And now I begin to understand why I was imprisoned so many years in this lonely chamber, and why I could never break through the viewless bolts and bars; for if I had sooner made my escape into the world, I should have grown hard and rough, and been covered with earthly dust, and my heart might have become callous by rude encounters with the multitude. . . . But living in solitude till the fulness of time was come, I still kept the dew of my youth and the freshness of my heart. . . . I used to think I could imagine all passions, all feelings, and states of the heart and mind; but how little did I know! . . . . Indeed, we are but shadows; we are not endowed with real life, and all that seems most real about us is but the thinnest substance of a dream,—till the heart be touched. That touch creates us,—then we begin to be,—thereby we are beings of reality and inheritors of eternity. . . .

When we shall be endowed with our spiritual bodies, I think that they will be so constituted that we may send thoughts and feelings any distance in no time at all, and transfuse them warm and fresh into the consciousness of those whom we love. . . . But, after all, perhaps it is not wise to intermix fantastic ideas with the reality of affection. Let us content ourselves to be earthly creatures, and hold communion of spirit in such modes as are ordained to us. . . .

I was not at the end of Long Wharf to-day, but in a distant region,—my authority having been put in requisition to quell a rebellion of the captain and "gang" of shovellers aboard a coal-vessel. I would you could have beheld the awful sternness of my visage and demeanor in the execution of this momentous duty. Well,—I have conquered the rebels, and proclaimed an amnesty; so to-morrow I shall return to that paradise of measurers, the end of Long Wharf,—not to my former salt-ship, she being now discharged, but to another, which will probably employ me well-nigh a fortnight longer. . . . Salt is white and pure,—there is something holy in salt. . . .

I have observed that butterflies—very broad-winged and magnificent butterflies—frequently come on board of the salt-ship, where I am at work. What have these bright strangers to do on Long Wharf, where there are no flowers nor any green thing,—nothing but brick storehouses, stone piers, black ships, and the bustle of toilsome men, who neither look up to the blue sky, nor take note of these wandering gems of the air? I cannot account for them, unless they are the lovely fantasies of the mind.

November.—. . . . How delightfully long the evenings are now! I do not get intolerably tired any longer; and my thoughts sometimes wander back to literature, and I have momentary impulses to write stories. But this will not be at present. The utmost that I can hope to do will be to portray some of the characteristics of the life which I am now living, and of the people with whom I am brought into contact, for future use. . . . The days are cold now, the air eager and nipping, yet it suits my health amazingly. I feel as if I could run a hundred miles at a stretch, and jump over all the houses that happen to be in my way. . . .

I have never had the good luck to profit much, or indeed any, by attending lectures, so that I think the ticket had better be bestowed on somebody who can listen to Mr. ——— more worthily. My evenings are very precious to me, and some of them are unavoidably thrown away in paying or receiving visits, or in writing letters of business, and therefore I prize the rest as if the sands of the hour-glass were gold or diamond dust.

I was invited to dine at Mr. Baucroft's yesterday with Miss Margaret Fuller; but Providence had given me some business to do, for which I was very thankful.

Is not this a beautiful morning? The sun shines into my soul.

April, 1841.—. . . . I have been busy all day, from early breakfast-time till late in the afternoon; and old Father Time has gone onward somewhat less heavily than is his wont when I am imprisoned within the walls of the Custom-House. It has been a brisk, breezy day, an effervescent atmosphere, and I have enjoyed it in all its freshness,—breathing air which had not been breathed in advance by the hundred thousand pairs of lungs which have common and indivisible property in the atmosphere of this great city. My breath had never belonged to anybody but me. It came fresh from the wilderness of ocean. . . . It was exhilarating to see the vessels, how they bounded over the waves, while a sheet of foam broke out around them. I found a good deal of enjoyment, too, in the busy scene around me; for several vessels were disgorging themselves (what an unseemly figure is this,—"disgorge," quotha, as if the vessels were sick) on the wharf, and everybody seemed to be working with might and main. It pleased me to think that I also had a part to act in the material and tangible business of this life, and that a portion of all this industry could not have gone on without my presence. Nevertheless, I must not pride myself too much on my activity and utilitarianism. I shall, doubtless, soon bewail myself at being compelled to earn my bread by taking some little share in the toils of mortal men. . . .

Articulate words are a harsh clamor and dissonance. When man arrives at his highest perfection, he will again be dumb! for I suppose he was dumb at the Creation, and must go round an entire circle in order to return to that blessed state.

END OF VOL. I

About Author

Nathaniel Hawthorne (Hathorne; July 4, 1804 – May 19, 1864) was an American novelist, dark romantic, and short story writer. His works often focus on history, morality, and religion.

He was born in 1804 in Salem, Massachusetts, to Nathaniel Hathorne and the former Elizabeth Clarke Manning. His ancestors include John Hathorne, the only judge involved in the Salem witch trials who never repented of his actions. He entered Bowdoin College in 1821, was elected to Phi Beta Kappa in 1824, and graduated in 1825. He published his first work in 1828, the novel Fanshawe; he later tried to suppress it, feeling that it was not equal to the standard of his later work. He published several short stories in periodicals, which he collected in 1837 as Twice-Told Tales. The next year, he became engaged to Sophia Peabody. He worked at the Boston Custom House and joined Brook Farm, a transcendentalist community, before marrying Peabody in 1842. The couple moved to The Old Manse in Concord, Massachusetts, later moving to Salem, the Berkshires, then to The Wayside in Concord. The Scarlet Letter was published in 1850, followed by a succession of other novels. A political appointment as consul took Hawthorne and family to Europe before their return to Concord in 1860. Hawthorne died on May 19, 1864, and was survived by his wife and their three children.

Much of Hawthorne's writing centers on New England, many works featuring moral metaphors with an anti-Puritan inspiration. His fiction works are considered part of the Romantic movement and, more specifically, dark romanticism. His themes often center on the inherent evil and sin of humanity, and his works often have moral messages and deep psychological complexity. His published works include novels, short stories, and a biography of his college friend Franklin Pierce, the 14th President of the United States.

Biography

Early life

Nathaniel Hawthorne was born on July 4, 1804, in Salem, Massachusetts;

his birthplace is preserved and open to the public. William Hathorne was the author's great-great-great-grandfather. He was a Puritan and was the first of the family to emigrate from England, settling in Dorchester, Massachusetts, before moving to Salem. There he became an important member of the Massachusetts Bay Colony and held many political positions, including magistrate and judge, becoming infamous for his harsh sentencing. William's son and the author's great-great-grandfather John Hathorne was one of the judges who oversaw the Salem witch trials. Hawthorne probably added the "w" to his surname in his early twenties, shortly after graduating from college, in an effort to dissociate himself from his notorious forebears. Hawthorne's father Nathaniel Hathorne Sr. was a sea captain who died in 1808 of yellow fever in Suriname; he had been a member of the East India Marine Society. After his death, his widow moved with young Nathaniel and two daughters to live with relatives named the Mannings in Salem, where they lived for 10 years. Young Hawthorne was hit on the leg while playing "bat and ball" on November 10, 1813, and he became lame and bedridden for a year, though several physicians could find nothing wrong with him.

In the summer of 1816, the family lived as boarders with farmers before moving to a home recently built specifically for them by Hawthorne's uncles Richard and Robert Manning in Raymond, Maine, near Sebago Lake. Years later, Hawthorne looked back at his time in Maine fondly: "Those were delightful days, for that part of the country was wild then, with only scattered clearings, and nine tenths of it primeval woods." In 1819, he was sent back to Salem for school and soon complained of homesickness and being too far from his mother and sisters. He distributed seven issues of The Spectator to his family in August and September 1820 for the sake of having fun. The homemade newspaper was written by hand and included essays, poems, and news featuring the young author's adolescent humor.

Hawthorne's uncle Robert Manning insisted that the boy attend college, despite Hawthorne's protests. With the financial support of his uncle, Hawthorne was sent to Bowdoin College in 1821, partly because of family connections in the area, and also because of its relatively inexpensive tuition rate. Hawthorne met future president Franklin Pierce on the way to

Bowdoin, at the stage stop in Portland, and the two became fast friends. Once at the school, he also met future poet Henry Wadsworth Longfellow, future congressman Jonathan Cilley, and future naval reformer Horatio Bridge. He graduated with the class of 1825, and later described his college experience to Richard Henry Stoddard:

> I was educated (as the phrase is) at Bowdoin College. I was an idle student, negligent of college rules and the Procrustean details of academic life, rather choosing to nurse my own fancies than to dig into Greek roots and be numbered among the learned Thebans.

Early career

In 1836, Hawthorne served as the editor of the American Magazine of Useful and Entertaining Knowledge. At the time, he boarded with poet Thomas Green Fessenden on Hancock Street in Beacon Hill in Boston. He was offered an appointment as weigher and gauger at the Boston Custom House at a salary of $1,500 a year, which he accepted on January 17, 1839. During his time there, he rented a room from George Stillman Hillard, business partner of Charles Sumner. Hawthorne wrote in the comparative obscurity of what he called his "owl's nest" in the family home. As he looked back on this period of his life, he wrote: "I have not lived, but only dreamed about living." He contributed short stories to various magazines and annuals, including "Young Goodman Brown" and "The Minister's Black Veil", though none drew major attention to him. Horatio Bridge offered to cover the risk of collecting these stories in the spring of 1837 into the volume Twice-Told Tales, which made Hawthorne known locally.

Marriage and family

While at Bowdoin, Hawthorne wagered a bottle of Madeira wine with his friend Jonathan Cilley that Cilley would get married before Hawthorne did. By 1836, he had won the bet, but he did not remain a bachelor for life. He had public flirtations with Mary Silsbee and Elizabeth Peabody, then he began pursuing Peabody's sister, illustrator and transcendentalist Sophia Peabody. He joined the transcendentalist Utopian community at Brook Farm in 1841, not because he agreed with the experiment but because it helped him save money to marry Sophia. He paid a $1,000 deposit and was put in charge of shoveling the hill of manure referred to as "the Gold Mine". He left later that year, though his Brook Farm adventure became an inspiration for his novel The Blithedale Romance. Hawthorne married Sophia Peabody on July 9, 1842, at a ceremony in the Peabody parlor on West Street in Boston. The couple moved to The Old Manse in Concord, Massachusetts, where they lived for three years. His neighbor Ralph Waldo Emerson invited him into his social circle, but Hawthorne was almost pathologically shy and stayed silent at gatherings. At the Old Manse, Hawthorne wrote most of the tales collected in Mosses from an Old Manse.

Like Hawthorne, Sophia was a reclusive person. Throughout her early life, she had frequent migraines and underwent several experimental medical treatments. She was mostly bedridden until her sister introduced her to Hawthorne, after which her headaches seem to have abated. The Hawthornes enjoyed a long and happy marriage. He referred to her as his "Dove" and wrote that she "is, in the strictest sense, my sole companion; and I need no other—there is no vacancy in my mind, any more than in my heart ... Thank God that I suffice for her boundless heart!" Sophia greatly admired her husband's work. She wrote in one of her journals:

> I am always so dazzled and bewildered with the richness, the depth, the ... jewels of beauty in his productions that I am always looking forward to a second reading where I can ponder and muse and fully take in the miraculous wealth of thoughts.

Poet Ellery Channing came to the Old Manse for help on the first anniversary of the Hawthornes' marriage. A local teenager named Martha Hunt had drowned herself in the river and Hawthorne's boat Pond Lily was needed to find her body. Hawthorne helped recover the corpse, which he described as "a spectacle of such perfect horror ... She was the very image of death-agony". The incident later inspired a scene in his novel The Blithedale Romance.

The Hawthornes had three children. Their first was daughter Una born March 3, 1844; her name was a reference to The Faerie Queene, to the displeasure of family members. Hawthorne wrote to a friend, "I find it a very sober and serious kind of happiness that springs from the birth of a child ... There is no escaping it any longer. I have business on earth now, and must look about me for the means of doing it." In October 1845, the Hawthornes moved to Salem. In 1846, their son Julian was born. Hawthorne wrote to his sister Louisa on June 22, 1846: "A small troglodyte made his appearance here at ten minutes to six o'clock this morning, who claimed to be your nephew." Daughter Rose was born in May 1851, and Hawthorne called her his "autumnal flower".

Middle years

In April 1846, Hawthorne was officially appointed the Surveyor for the District of Salem and Beverly and Inspector of the Revenue for the Port of Salem at an annual salary of $1,200. He had difficulty writing during this period, as he admitted to Longfellow:

> I am trying to resume my pen ... Whenever I sit alone, or walk alone, I find myself dreaming about stories, as of old; but these forenoons in the Custom House undo all that the afternoons and evenings have done. I should be happier if I could write.

This employment, like his earlier appointment to the custom house in Boston, was vulnerable to the politics of the spoils system. Hawthorne was a Democrat and lost this job due to the change of administration in Washington after the presidential election of 1848. He wrote a letter of protest to the Boston Daily Advertiser which was attacked by the Whigs and supported by the Democrats, making Hawthorne's dismissal a much-talked about event in New England. He was deeply affected by the death of his mother in late July, calling it "the darkest hour I ever lived". He was appointed the corresponding secretary of the Salem Lyceum in 1848. Guests who came to speak that season included Emerson, Thoreau, Louis Agassiz, and Theodore Parker.

Hawthorne returned to writing and published The Scarlet Letter in mid-March 1850, including a preface that refers to his three-year tenure in the Custom House and makes several allusions to local politicians—who did not appreciate their treatment. It was one of the first mass-produced books in America, selling 2,500 volumes within ten days and earning Hawthorne $1,500 over 14 years. The book was pirated by booksellers in London and became a best-seller in the United States; it initiated his most lucrative period as a writer. Hawthorne's friend Edwin Percy Whipple objected to the novel's "morbid intensity" and its dense psychological details, writing that the book "is therefore apt to become, like Hawthorne, too painfully anatomical in his exhibition of them", though 20th-century writer D. H. Lawrence said that there could be no more perfect work of the American imagination than The Scarlet Letter.

Hawthorne and his family moved to a small red farmhouse near Lenox, Massachusetts, at the end of March 1850. He became friends with Herman Melville beginning on August 5, 1850, when the authors met at a picnic hosted by a mutual friend. Melville had just read Hawthorne's short story collection Mosses from an Old Manse, and his unsigned review of the collection was printed in The Literary World on August 17 and August 24 titled "Hawthorne and His Mosses". Melville wrote that these stories revealed a dark side to Hawthorne, "shrouded in blackness, ten times black". He was composing his novel Moby-Dick at the time, and dedicated the work in 1851 to Hawthorne: "In token of my admiration for his genius, this book is inscribed to Nathaniel Hawthorne."

Hawthorne's time in the Berkshires was very productive. While there, he wrote The House of the Seven Gables (1851), which poet and critic James Russell Lowell said was better than The Scarlet Letter and called "the most valuable contribution to New England history that has been made." He also wrote The Blithedale Romance (1852), his only work written in the first person. He also published A Wonder-Book for Girls and Boys in 1851, a collection of short stories retelling myths which he had been thinking about writing since 1846. Nevertheless, poet Ellery Channing reported that Hawthorne "has suffered much living in this place". The family enjoyed the scenery of the Berkshires, although Hawthorne did not enjoy the winters in their small house. They left on November 21, 1851. Hawthorne noted, "I am sick to death of Berkshire ... I have felt languid and dispirited, during almost my whole residence."

The Wayside and Europe

In May 1852, the Hawthornes returned to Concord where they lived until July 1853. In February, they bought The Hillside, a home previously inhabited by Amos Bronson Alcott and his family, and renamed it The Wayside. Their neighbors in Concord included Emerson and Henry David Thoreau. That year, Hawthorne wrote The Life of Franklin Pierce, the campaign biography of his friend which depicted him as "a man of peaceful pursuits". Horace Mann said, "If he makes out Pierce to be a great man or a brave man, it will be the greatest work of fiction he ever wrote." In the biography, Hawthorne depicts Pierce as a statesman and soldier who had accomplished no great feats because of his need to make "little noise" and so "withdrew into the background". He also left out Pierce's drinking habits, despite rumors of his alcoholism, and emphasized Pierce's belief that slavery could not "be remedied by human contrivances" but would, over time, "vanish like a dream".

With Pierce's election as President, Hawthorne was rewarded in 1853 with the position of United States consul in Liverpool shortly after the publication of Tanglewood Tales. The role was considered the most lucrative foreign service position at the time, described by Hawthorne's wife as "second in dignity to the Embassy in London". His appointment ended in 1857 at the close of the Pierce administration, and the Hawthorne family toured France and Italy. During his time in Italy, the previously clean-shaven Hawthorne grew a bushy mustache.

The family returned to The Wayside in 1860, and that year saw the publication of The Marble Faun, his first new book in seven years. Hawthorne admitted that he had aged considerably, referring to himself as "wrinkled with time and trouble".

Later years and death

At the outset of the American Civil War, Hawthorne traveled with William D. Ticknor to Washington, D.C., where he met Abraham Lincoln and other notable figures. He wrote about his experiences in the essay "Chiefly About War Matters" in 1862.

Failing health prevented him from completing several more romance novels. Hawthorne was suffering from pain in his stomach and insisted on a recuperative trip with his friend Franklin Pierce, though his neighbor Bronson Alcott was concerned that Hawthorne was too ill. While on a tour of the White Mountains, he died in his sleep on May 19, 1864, in Plymouth, New Hampshire. Pierce sent a telegram to Elizabeth Peabody asking her to inform Mrs. Hawthorne in person. Mrs. Hawthorne was too saddened by the news to handle the funeral arrangements herself. Hawthorne's son Julian was a freshman at Harvard College, and he learned of his father's death the next day; coincidentally, he was initiated into the Delta Kappa Epsilon fraternity on the same day by being blindfolded and placed in a coffin.Longfellow wrote a tribute poem to Hawthorne published in 1866 called "The Bells of Lynn". Hawthorne was buried on what is now known as "Authors' Ridge" in Sleepy Hollow Cemetery, Concord, Massachusetts. Pallbearers included Longfellow, Emerson, Alcott, Oliver Wendell Holmes Sr., James Thomas Fields, and Edwin Percy Whipple. Emerson wrote of the funeral: "I thought there was a tragic element in the event, that might be more fully rendered—in the painful solitude of the man, which, I suppose, could no longer be endured, & he died of it."

His wife Sophia and daughter Una were originally buried in England. However, in June 2006, they were reinterred in plots adjacent to Hawthorne.

Writings

Hawthorne had a particularly close relationship with his publishers William Ticknor and James Thomas Fields. Hawthorne once told Fields, "I care more for your good opinion than for that of a host of critics." In fact, it was Fields who convinced Hawthorne to turn The Scarlet Letter into a novel rather than a short story. Ticknor handled many of Hawthorne's personal matters, including the purchase of cigars, overseeing financial accounts and even purchasing clothes. Ticknor died with Hawthorne at his side in Philadelphia in 1864; according to a friend, Hawthorne was left "apparently dazed".

Literary style and themes

Hawthorne's works belong to romanticism or, more specifically, dark romanticism, cautionary tales that suggest that guilt, sin, and evil are the most inherent natural qualities of humanity. Many of his works are inspired by Puritan New England, combining historical romance loaded with symbolism and deep psychological themes, bordering on surrealism. His depictions of the past are a version of historical fiction used only as a vehicle to express common themes of ancestral sin, guilt and retribution. His later writings also reflect his negative view of the Transcendentalism movement.

Hawthorne was predominantly a short story writer in his early career. Upon publishing Twice-Told Tales, however, he noted, "I do not think much of them," and he expected little response from the public. His four major romances were written between 1850 and 1860: The Scarlet Letter (1850), The House of the Seven Gables (1851), The Blithedale Romance (1852) and The Marble Faun (1860). Another novel-length romance, Fanshawe, was published anonymously in 1828. Hawthorne defined a romance as being radically different from a novel by not being concerned with the possible or probable course of ordinary experience. In the preface to The House of the Seven Gables, Hawthorne describes his romance-writing as using "atmospherical medium as to bring out or mellow the lights and deepen and enrich the shadows of the picture". The picture, Daniel Hoffman found, was one of "the primitive energies of fecundity and creation."

Critics have applied feminist perspectives and historicist approaches to Hawthorne's depictions of women. Feminist scholars are interested particularly in Hester Prynne: they recognize that while she herself could not be the "destined prophetess" of the future, the "angel and apostle of the coming revelation" must nevertheless "be a woman." Camille Paglia saw Hester as mystical, "a wandering goddess still bearing the mark of her Asiatic origins ... moving serenely in the magic circle of her sexual nature". Lauren Berlant termed Hester "the citizen as woman [personifying] love as a quality of the body that contains the purest light of nature," her resulting "traitorous political theory" a "Female Symbolic" literalization of futile Puritan metaphors. Historicists view Hester as a protofeminist and avatar of the self-reliance and responsibility that led to women's suffrage and reproductive emancipation. Anthony Splendora found her literary genealogy among other archetypally fallen but redeemed women, both historic and mythic. As examples, he offers Psyche of ancient legend; Heloise of twelfth-century France's tragedy involving world-renowned philosopher Peter Abelard; Anne Hutchinson (America's first heretic, circa 1636), and Hawthorne family friend Margaret Fuller. In Hester's first appearance, Hawthorne likens her, "infant at her bosom", to Mary, Mother of Jesus, "the image of Divine Maternity". In her study of Victorian literature, in which such "galvanic outcasts" as Hester feature prominently, Nina Auerbach went so far as to name Hester's fall and subsequent redemption, "the novel's one unequivocally religious activity". Regarding Hester as a deity figure, Meredith A. Powers found in Hester's characterization "the earliest in American fiction that the archetypal Goddess appears quite graphically," like a Goddess "not the wife of traditional marriage, permanently subject to a male overlord"; Powers noted "her syncretism, her flexibility, her inherent ability to alter and so avoid the defeat of secondary status in a goal-oriented civilization".

Aside from Hester Prynne, the model women of Hawthorne's other novels—from Ellen Langton of Fanshawe to Zenobia and Priscilla of The Blithedale Romance, Hilda and Miriam of The Marble Faun and Phoebe and Hepzibah of The House of the Seven Gables—are more fully realized than his male characters, who merely orbit them. This observation is equally true of his short-stories, in which central females serve as allegorical figures: Rappaccini's beautiful but life-altering, garden-bound, daughter; almost-perfect Georgiana of "The Birthmark"; the sinned-against (abandoned) Ester of "Ethan Brand"; and goodwife Faith Brown, linchpin of Young Goodman Brown's very belief in God. "My Faith is gone!" Brown exclaims in despair upon seeing his wife at the Witches' Sabbath. Perhaps the most sweeping statement of Hawthorne's impetus comes from Mark Van Doren: "Somewhere, if not in the New England of his time, Hawthorne unearthed the image of a goddess supreme in beauty and power."

Hawthorne also wrote nonfiction. In 2008, the Library of America selected Hawthorne's "A show of wax-figures" for inclusion in its two-century retrospective of American True Crime.

Criticism

In "Hawthorne and His Mosses", Herman Melville wrote a passionate argument for Hawthorne to be among the burgeoning American literary canon, "He is one of the new, and far better generation of your writers." In this review of Mosses from an Old Manse, Melville describes an affinity for Hawthorne that would only increase: "I feel that this Hawthorne has dropped germinous seeds into my soul. He expands and deepens down, the more I contemplate him; and further, and further, shoots his strong New-England roots into the hot soil of my Southern soul." Edgar Allan Poe wrote important reviews of both Twice-Told Tales and Mosses from an Old Manse. Poe's assessment was partly informed by his contempt of allegory and moral tales, and his chronic accusations of plagiarism, though he admitted,

> The style of Mr. Hawthorne is purity itself. His tone is singularly effective—wild, plaintive, thoughtful, and in full accordance with his themes ... We look upon him as one of the few men of indisputable genius to whom our country has as yet given birth.

Ralph Waldo Emerson wrote, "Nathaniel Hawthorne's reputation as a writer is a very pleasing fact, because his writing is not good for anything, and this is a tribute to the man." Henry James praised Hawthorne, saying, "The fine thing in Hawthorne is that he cared for the deeper psychology, and that, in his way, he tried to become familiar with it." Poet John Greenleaf Whittier wrote that he admired the "weird and subtle beauty" in Hawthorne's tales. Evert Augustus Duyckinck said of Hawthorne, "Of the American writers destined to live, he is the most original, the one least indebted to foreign models or literary precedents of any kind."

Contemporary response to Hawthorne's work praised his sentimentality and moral purity while more modern evaluations focus on the dark psychological complexity. Beginning in the 1950s, critics have focused on symbolism and didacticism.

The critic Harold Bloom opined that only Henry James and William Faulkner challenge Hawthorne's position as the greatest American novelist, although he admitted that he favored James as the greatest American novelist.

Bloom saw Hawthorne's greatest works to be principally The Scarlet Letter, followed by The Marble Faun and certain short stories, including "My Kinsman, Major Molineux", "Young Goodman Brown", "Wakefield", and "Feathertop". (Source: Wikipedia)

NOTABLE WORKS

NOVELS

Fanshawe (published anonymously, 1828)

The Scarlet Letter (1850)

The House of the Seven Gables (1851)

The Blithedale Romance (1852)

The Marble Faun: Or, The Romance of Monte Beni (1860) (as Transformation: Or, The Romance of Monte Beni, UK publication, same year)

The Dolliver Romance (1863) (unfinished)

Septimius Felton; or, the Elixir of Life (unfinished, published in the Atlantic Monthly, 1872)

Doctor Grimshawe's Secret: A Romance (unfinished, with preface and notes by Julian Hawthorne, 1882)

SHORT STORY COLLECTIONS

Twice-Told Tales (1837)

Grandfather's Chair (1840)

Mosses from an Old Manse (1846)

A Wonder-Book for Girls and Boys (1851)

The Snow-Image, and Other Twice-Told Tales (1852)

Tanglewood Tales (1853)

The Dolliver Romance and Other Pieces (1876)

The Great Stone Face and Other Tales of the White Mountains (1889)

SELECTED SHORT STORIES

"The Hollow of the Three Hills" (1830)

"Roger Malvin's Burial" (1832)

"My Kinsman, Major Molineux" (1832)

"The Minister's Black Veil" (1832)

"Young Goodman Brown" (1835)

"The Gray Champion" (1835)

"The White Old Maid" (1835)

"Wakefield" (1835)

"The Ambitious Guest" (1835)

"The Man of Adamant" (1837)

"The May-Pole of Merry Mount" (1837)

"The Great Carbuncle" (1837)

"Dr. Heidegger's Experiment" (1837)

"A Virtuoso's Collection" (May 1842)

"The Birth-Mark" (March 1843)

"The Celestial Railroad" (1843)

"Egotism; or, The Bosom-Serpent" (1843)

"Earth's Holocaust" (1844)

"Rappaccini's Daughter" (1844)

"P.'s Correspondence" (1845)

"The Artist of the Beautiful" (1846)

"Fire Worship" (1846)

"Ethan Brand" (1850)

"The Great Stone Face" (1850)

"Feathertop" (1852)

NONFICTION

Twenty Days with Julian & Little Bunny (written 1851, published 1904)

Our Old Home (1863)

Passages from the French and Italian Notebooks (1871)

CPSIA information can be obtained
at www.ICGtesting.com
Printed in the USA
LVHW050110140720
660559LV00004B/443